BUCKINGHAMSHIRE
MURDER
& CRIME

BUCKINGHAMSHIRE
MURDER
& CRIME

SCOTT HOUGHTON

The
History
Press

First published 2014

The History Press
The Mill, Brimscombe Port
Stroud, Gloucestershire, GL5 2QG
www.thehistorypress.co.uk

British Library Cataloguing in Publication Data.
A catalogue record for this book is available from the British Library.

ISBN 978 0 7524 8770 0

Typesetting and origination by The History Press
Printed in Great Britain

CONTENTS

ACKNOWLEDGEMENTS

I would like to express my gratitude to the following people who have all contributed to the completion of this book in their own way: Catherine Houghton, for her endurance during the long hours of research and her understanding when frustration besieged me; Ed Grimsdale, a legend and mentor for aspiring historians; the staff at the Centre for Buckinghamshire Studies, for their invaluable assistance; the *Bucks Herald*, for their creditable journalism; Ian Costar; Pam Reed; and Danielle Robson at Slough Library.

INTRODUCTION

When I decided to write this book I had anticipated fewer capital crimes and more crimes of a milder nature. The murders I have covered tend to be committed in a sudden frenzy of violence, often in an attempt to prevent the victim from identifying their attacker for a much lesser crime than that of murder. The favoured weapon is the knife which can be perceived as a somewhat 'personal' weapon to kill with; a more 'personal' way to murder. If one were to shoot somebody or poison them say, the murderer would be quite disassociated from the victim and could achieve their aim from a distance. When inflicting wounds with a knife, the perpetrator is close to the victim. The knife becomes an extension of the body, replicating each fluid and deliberate movement of the arm. The murderer is invariably contaminated with the blood of their victim, can hear their desperate cries for help, see the terror in their eyes, and witness their last gasp for breath.

The murderers in this book were all hanged in Aylesbury. The crimes were committed in the Aylesbury area and the accused (with two exceptions) were tried at the Aylesbury Assizes. Until 1810, hangings were conducted at Stone Bridge, nicknamed 'Gallows Bridge', just outside of the parish boundary on a site that now forms part of the Bicester Road. This meant conveying prisoners some distance, so executions from 1810 were carried out in the town: first outside the County Hall (now the County Court) then outside Aylesbury Gaol (the current Aylesbury Prison) until an act was passed in 1868 prohibiting public executions. From this time all further executions took place inside the gaol on a site which is now simply a lawn.

I have recounted the murders to include the inquests, trials and executions as these provide a fuller account of the circumstances surrounding the crimes and on what grounds the suspects were convicted and subsequently hanged.

It was not until the 1880s that defendants at trials were allowed to give evidence in their defence or under cross-examination and even then it was only permissable for certain crimes. In 1898, however, the defendants were allowed to give evidence at their own trial regardless of the crime.

I have attempted to include as many names as possible of the people involved in these crimes and the places they lived, so those of you who are interested in genealogy can maybe trace a good or bad ancestor. Which will yours be?

Scott Houghton, 2012

CASE ONE   1837

'MY DAYS ARE GONE LIKE A SHADOW'

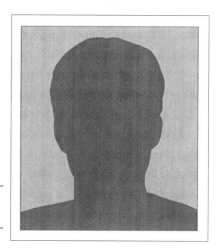

Soulbury, Heath and Reach

Suspect:	Thomas Bates
Age:	22
Charge:	Murder

Shortly after ten o'clock on the morning of Tuesday, 30 August 1836, and after an hour's searching, Jonathan Chew – gardener to Colonel Hanmer the then MP for Stockgrove, Buckinghamshire – discovered the corpse of his colleague, James Giltrow, abandoned in a copse on the west side of Bragenham Warren, situated between Leighton Buzzard and Great Brickhill.

Until his untimely demise, James Giltrow had been in the employ of Colonel Hanmer as his gamekeeper. Giltrow had not returned home from work the previous evening, causing his concerned wife to raise

'the corpse of his colleague'

the alarm early the following morning when she travelled to Stockgrove House, the home of Colonel Hanmer. As Giltrow was a gamekeeper it was perfectly feasible that he may work at night, hence why the alarm was not raised until the following morning.

When Chew discovered his colleague's lifeless remains he was initially unable to identify him as his face had been so battered and mutilated no discernible features remained.

Giltrow's identity was established by the presence of his shot belt, clothes and his still-loaded double-barrelled shot gun that lay alongside him. Chew raised the alarm and people rushed to the scene. First to arrive were some labourers who had been working in the adjoining fields owned by Mr Mortimer. Shortly afterwards they were joined by the inhabitants of the surrounding towns and villages.

The first constable to arrive was handed a discarded broken gunstock found at the scene, which peculiarly had a wax end. He immediately recognised it as belonging to Thomas Bates, from whom he had once borrowed the gun from which the gunstock came. Bates, aged twenty-two, was a labourer at the time of the murder and resided in Heath with his wife and two children. Knowing Bates was in employment on the railway nearby, the constable went at once to arrest and despatch him to Soulbury, where he would remain in custody until his trial. Initially, Bates denied knowledge of the gunstock or the murder of James Giltrow. However, it was not long before he confessed to the crime of which he stood accused.

Stockgrove: Colonel Hanmer's estate where Thomas Bates was caught poaching. (Author's collection)

Bates admitted that on Monday evening he had gone to Six Acre Wood in order to shoot rabbits, but while sitting on a gate he noticed a cock pheasant. He shot at and hit the pheasant but it was not killed and managed to escape. Bates then went through the warren into a corn stubble field under Chew's charge and concealed himself beneath a hedge. However, the gamekeeper James Giltrow appeared almost immediately, running towards Bates as fast as he could. Bates ducked back through the hedge and attempted to conceal himself in a ditch but was soon discovered by Giltrow who, according to Bates, said, 'I have looked for you many times and now I have you.' At first, Bates refused to leave his hiding place but soon realised he had been discovered and surrendered himself to Giltrow's mercy.

Bates claimed he told Giltrow, 'it is the first time you have caught me, and I hope you will forgive me.' Giltrow was unimpressed with this plea and insisted the poacher accompany him to the authorities. They set off together but before long Bates was confronted with the opportunity to escape and knocked Giltrow to the ground using the butt of his gun.

The staggering ferocity of the blow to the hapless Giltrow caused Bates' gun to break into three separate pieces. He attacked Giltrow's face and head with the barrel and then the lock of the broken gun.

Upon cessation of the frenzied attack, Bates was only able to recover two parts of his broken gun. The butt with the distinctive wax end could not be found, so Bates hid the remaining pieces, including the final butt piece and the barrel, in the nearby Rushmere Pond.

Bates returned home and retired to his bed around eight-thirty that evening. He rose at five o'clock the following morning to hunt for the remaining piece of the gun which would ultimately lead to his identification, trial and execution. Fortunately the moon was bright, enabling Bates to search for an hour. Although he was able to find many splintered shards of his gun he was unable to locate the incriminating piece that would identify him as Giltrow's murderer. He even rolled Giltrow's cold and bloodied corpse over to see if the slain man concealed the errant weapon part, but to no avail. Concerned he would be discovered near his victim and that the body was exposed, Bates pulled a stake from the hedge and laid it over the body. Unsatisfied in his quest to find the gun piece, he then made off for work as usual.

Rushmere Pond, where Thomas Bates hid the pieces of the murder weapon.
(Author's collection)

It was a cruel trick of fate for Bates that he had been unable to locate the missing gun piece, for when the crowds arrived upon the scene a few hours later, the distinctive butt was discovered almost immediately just yards from the body.

On Wednesday, 31 August 1836, just two days after the murder, the coroner's inquest was conducted at The Boot public house in Soulbury, under the direction of the coroner, J.W. Cowley, surgeon Dr Penrose, and an appointed jury.

Several witnesses were called upon who gave evidence that they had seen Thomas Bates in the vicinity of the copse around the time of the murder. One Bernard Fossey, just fourteen years old, confirmed that he had seen Bates between seven and eight o'clock at Baker's Wood.

Bates was granted permission to speak to his wife, whereupon he fell to tears and promised he 'would tell all about it'. Bates went on to confess his crime to the coroner's court and the case was adjourned until the following morning.

The Boot, Soulbury, where the coroner's inquest was held. (Author's collection)

When the court reconvened on Thursday morning, the two pieces of the gun Bates had concealed at Rushmere Pond had been recovered and were identified as belonging to him. Bates declared that no one had abetted or aided him during the crime and he had no malice aforethought. The jury took little time in declaring a verdict of 'wilful murder' and Bates was relayed to Aylesbury Gaol to await trial at the Lent County Assizes.

March 1837 saw the beginning of the trial of Thomas Bates for the murder of John Giltrow, before Justice Allan Park. Surprisingly, considering he had previously confessed to the crime at the coroner's inquest, Bates pleaded not guilty and challenged various members of the jury.

Messrs Storks and Roberts led the prosecution, while Mr Byles conducted the defence.

Bernard Fossey, the boy who had given evidence at the coroner's court, first gave his evidence that he had seen Bates at Baker's Wood on Monday 29 August at half past seven in the evening. Jonathan Chew, who had discovered Giltrow's battered corpse, was the next called to give his evidence.

Baker's Wood, where Thomas Bates was spotted on the evening of the murder.
(Author's collection)

Chew described how he found the dead and mutilated body of his colleague at around ten o'clock on the morning of 30 August.

Giltrow's stiff and cold body was lying on its back with the head a little to the left. His gun lay to the side and a large pointed hedge stake was between the body and the gun. After inspecting the stake, he noticed it was daubed in blood at the pointed end. He also remarked that Giltrow's right eye had popped out. The corner of the warren where the body lay was covered with high fern and oak trees whose boughs almost touched the ground; the body was concealed quite naturally in this location.

After a lacklustre and probably futile cross-examination by Mr Byles, Bates' defence counsel, a carpenter by the name of John Adams took to the witness stand. Adams recounted going to the warren where Giltrow's body lay on the morning after the murder and finding the 'missing' part of Bates' gun. He described the wax end that was to lead to the identity of Bates and his complicity in this heinous crime. Bates' gun was then produced in court. Adams was with his friend at the time and witnessed the prisoner brought close to the warren and heard him deny that the gun was his. However, shortly afterwards, Adams heard Bates claim that he had hidden the remaining parts of the gun in a pond at Craddock's Spinney. They subsequently visited Craddock's Spinney with Bates but he claimed it was not there. The gun parts were recovered the following morning after Bates' confession at the coroner's inquest.

John Mortimer, a farmer from Heath and Reach, was then called and related how he had formerly employed Bates and identified the gun as belonging to him. He witnessed Bates in possession of that same gun on a number of occasions, the most recent being three or four weeks before Giltrow's death. Mortimer had remarked upon its danger as a weapon, such was its parlous state of repair. Mortimer then went on to recite how, at The Boot public house in Soulbury on the day after the murder, he had engaged in a conversation with Bates concerning the death of Giltrow. According to Mortimer's testimony, Bates confessed in great detail, describing the circumstances of the murder and how he viciously slaughtered his victim, as well as where he had hidden the broken gun parts he still had in his possession.

Mortimer was cross-examined by Mr Byles but it appears Byles made no real effort to uncover any detail that may spare his client from the hangman's noose. Indeed, more damning evidence was provided when Mortimer recounted a conversation he had with Bates some weeks prior to the murder of Giltrow in The Boot, where he had warned Bates that if he were to be caught in Mortimer's field he would be 'taken up'. Re-examined by the prosecution, Mortimer gave Bates' reply to this as, 'If I knew any man who would do so, or tell of me I would blow his brains out or knock them out.' Bates indeed kept his promise.

Following Mortimer on the witness stand was Thomas Henley who had stood guard over the arrested man at The Boot in Soulbury. Handcuffed to Bates, he witnessed a visit from Bates' wife on 31 August, two days after the murder. Following a tearful conversation with his wife, Bates confessed to killing Giltrow and warned others from poaching in the future. 'I am the man who killed Giltrow,' he had exclaimed.

This appears to have been Bates' fullest confession. He had gone to shoot a rabbit but saw a cock pheasant across the Six Acre turnip field. He hit the pheasant with a shot but it was not a fatal blow and the bird flew over into the warren. Instead of chasing the stricken bird, he decided to head for home by way of Bragenham Lane so if he should be seen by any passers-by they would simply assume he was returning from work on the railway.

Along the way, Bates saw Colonel Hanmer's gamekeeper, James Giltrow so he hid in a ditch in order to evade detection. However, Giltrow saw where he had attempted to conceal his person and confronted him regarding the shooting of the pheasant. Bates pleaded for forgiveness but Giltrow was aware that Bates had been poaching on a regular basis and had been troublesome to him in the past so sought to take him in.

According to Bates himself, Giltrow refused forgiveness but did still offer to do what he could for him. This kindness was to be repaid with a savage attack that left the victim so disfigured he was unrecognisable to those who knew him.

Giltrow, somewhat trustingly as Bates was armed with a loaded gun, led the way and it must be assumed then that he did not fear for his safety. Bates then set about Giltrow with his gun, not firing it which would have been a kindness as death may have been instantaneous, but striking Giltrow repeatedly around the head and face with such force that the gun shattered into numerous parts. The witness, Thomas Henley, told Bates that he could not imagine how he could continue striking the man once he was upon the ground. Bates replied that he had to ensure Giltrow was dead or else he would report him and provide evidence against him.

Henley continued: Bates had told him that after attacking Giltrow he had returned home, hiding the pieces of the gun under some rushes at the pond near the warren. After a sleepless night, he rose early and on the premise of leaving to collect some mushrooms, Bates returned to the crime scene expecting to find Giltrow still alive and to search for the missing gun part.

Does this mean Giltrow was still breathing when Bates left him at around eight o'clock the previous evening or was guilt and paranoia creeping into the man's mind?

Bragenham Lane – the route taken by Thomas Bates to avoid being spotted leaving Rushmere Pond. (Author's collection)

Bates knew that if he could not find the missing part of his gun with the distinctive wax end he would be undone. Unable to locate the missing piece, which was later found some 7 f from Giltrow's body, Bates entered one of Mortimer's adjacent fields and tore out a fence stake. He then smeared it with blood that had congealed around Giltrow's head wounds, in an effort to make it look like the stake was the murder weapon rather than the gun which would indicate his guilt.

Constable Thomas Hopkins of Heath & Reach gave evidence next. He confirmed that he had been present when Bates made the confession to John Mortimer, his former employer, at The Boot two days after the murder had taken place. He told the court how Bates was in his beer shop on the night of the murder with a Thomas Line. The men drank together until four o'clock when they left.

Hopkins then described how he visited the murder site on the morning of 30 August and was presented with the missing gun part that unmistakably implicated Bates. Constable Hopkins had borrowed the very same gun from Bates less than a fortnight before so he was able to identify the owner immediately. Hopkins' servant, Thomas Cook, also identified the gun, as it was he who had returned the gun to Bates after cleaning it and gave testimony to that effect.

Thomas Line, who had been drinking with Bates on the afternoon of the murder, was called next. He delivered some damning evidence about Bates' intentions. He was not aware Bates would use the gun to commit murder but he did describe how Bates wanted to smuggle the gun passed the village to engage in some poaching. Line accompanied Bates back to his house whereupon Bates produced the now-infamous gun. He asked Line to take the gun to town with him because he was a stranger and would go unnoticed, whereas Bates would draw attention as he was already known for his poaching habits. Line did as he was asked and met Bates on the common before Bates asked him to go on to Rushmere Pond.

Line described Bates' attire which consisted of a hat, brown smock, white cotton stockings and low shoes. When he saw Bates again the following morning, after the deadly deed had been perpetrated, he was in an entirely different outfit.

Further evidence regarding the gun and Bates' whereabouts was provided by Henry Stockton who witnessed Bates passing his house at Rushmere Pond with the gun in his hand. He identified the gun having also borrowed it from Bates some three weeks earlier.

Joseph Flint was despatched to search Bates' home and found the clothing described by Thomas Line, hidden and soiled by blood splatters.

Perhaps the final nail in the coffin for Bates' defence was the evidence given by Dr Penrose who had carried out the post-mortem examination. Penrose described the injuries to Giltrow's head saying there was a severe wound on the forehead and on the right-hand side of the head, with considerable loss of the frontal bone as if it had been beaten off. No bone in the skull remained unbroken with Penrose stating they were all very severely fractured. Penrose concluded a long narrative of the injuries he found by confirming that the wounds had most certainly been the cause of Giltrow's death. He suggested the injuries were made using two different weapons, those being consistent with the butt end and the lock of a gun.

Finally, Staniford Rowland took the witness stand. He had been responsible for searching the pond in order to recover the gun pieces concealed there by Bates after he had bludgeoned Giltrow to death. He confirmed he had found the pieces where Bates had confessed to hiding them. Under cross-examination from Mr Byles, Rowland confirmed he had 'never heard the least tittle amiss of him before this time'.

The prosecution rested in what was a simple case to adjudicate. Despite the not guilty plea by the defendant, he had previously confessed to the crime and there was a great deal of evidence confirming his guilt. Despite this, Mr Byles contested a capital charge with two arguments. The first was that James Giltrow had no right to apprehend Bates or any other poacher as he was not proven to have been a gamekeeper acting in an official capacity. Secondly, Byles argued that Bates had been illegally arrested and detained by Giltrow and was therefore acting in self-defence. It was an imaginative and clever defence but one which would prove futile.

The judge, Justice Allan Park, was unimpressed and declared that he believed no such arrest, illegal or otherwise, took place.

Several character witnesses were then brought before the court to testify to the defendant's former good character and Mr Byles addressed the jury but all this was in vain. Justice Allan Park donned the black cap and delivered a sentence of death upon Thomas Bates who continued to conduct himself in a placid and attentive manner.

Thomas Bates was resigned to his fate and bore no malice to those who condemned him to death as he shook hands with each prosecution witness. He claimed, 'This is only, and no more than what I expected and all is how it ought to be.'

Before he was conveyed to the scaffold Bates spent a peaceful evening in quiet contemplation of meeting his God. He refused alcohol for he now understood its evil influence and spent little time sleeping, grateful as he was to be allowed to view the stars once more. At six in the morning he consumed a modest breakfast of coffee and bread and butter before withdrawing to his sleeping area. Around seven o'clock he emerged and said he was ready.

One member of the congregation bade him farewell advising they should never meet again. Bates still retained his good humour and replied, 'Oh yes we shall meet again and, I hope, in a better place than this.'

County Hall, Aylesbury, outside which Thomas Bates was executed. (Author's collection)

Bates was asked if he was afraid to die and he replied with the self-deprecating, 'No, and that instead of being hung by the neck, if I were hung by the heels till I were dead, it would be nothing to what I deserved.'

At the time the murder was committed, Bates was illiterate but during his short incarceration of less than three weeks, pending execution, he learned how to read and write in order to find solace through the words of the Bible. Bates conducted himself admirably while he awaited his fate although he did appear subdued, as one might expect. However, rumours unfairly circulated and, subsequently, almost gathered credence that the condemned man behaved as a desensitised criminal.

While continuing to condemn Bates for his heinous crime, some commentators sought to defend him from the slanderous nature of these rumours. This was not an attempt to encourage public sympathy or even understanding, but merely to ensure the truth was broadcast and a matter for public record.

Indeed, Bates showed contrition and repentance, comforted as he was by the chaplain resident at Aylesbury Gaol. He hoped simply to serve his sentence in this world with resigned acceptance to be greeted with forgiveness in the next world.

Spectators would pay to watch the executions from the vantage point of The Green Man's balcony. (Author's collection)

Bates had pleaded not guilty in the vain hope of escaping the death penalty. Once convicted though, he refused to lie about the crime any further, even to his fellow convicts who reportedly treated him harshly. He would spend entire nights in prayer and wept frequently. These observations can be relied upon as a result of a thorough and constant watch of the condemned man. One might almost feel compassion for a man who had plainly erred and felt remorse for his terrible actions; however, the law in the 1830s dictated that he must face the death penalty. Is it enough to show remorse in order to have one's sentence commuted or even to be forgiven for a brutal act such as that perpetrated by Bates? After all, had he accompanied James Giltrow as requested, he would have faced a relatively short prison sentence at worst, rather than the death penalty that concluded this tragic man's life and deprived a wife of her husband. Ultimately, two family men were to lose their lives in barbaric fashion for the attempted theft of one pheasant.

St Leonard's, where James Giltrow was interred. (Author's collection)

St Leonard's graveyard. (Author's collection)

Whilst awaiting his fate, Thomas Bates composed a letter and a prayer for the female prisoners whom he had heard weep while hearing the last sermon he would ever hear in the gaol chapel. These are reproduced below:

Dear Sisters

It is a shameful thing to hear that sin has stolen my life away but I hope you will all be ruled by me. I heard you cry which I thought was for me. Dear sisters, I feel happy and if you will be ruled by me you will be happy. Dear sisters, this is what I hope you will do; keep from all sin and wicked men when you have your time again. This I say, seek the Lord while you have the liberty. O seek the Lord while he may be found, for yet you stand on praying ground. O dear sisters, take heed to my words, for the sake of your own souls. Again I say take the time of liberty for you know, as well as me, if to be that we die in our sins without true repentance, we must be lost in hell. God bless you all, I hope. Pray be ruled by me.

'My days are gone like a shadow by reason of my sin.'

Prayer for you to learn Dear Sisters:
O my God be merciful to me a sinner. Have mercy upon me O my God, after thy great goodness according to thy mercies deliver my soul from hell. O merciful God have mercy upon a miserable sinner for the sake of thy dear Son. O merciful God grant me true repentance. O teach me the way that pleases thee for that is my desire – to serve thee truly day and night for that is my desire. Lord grant me my request a shameful sinner that I am. To thee alone can I look for comfort or sure trust. In thee O Lord, I put my trust. O grant me my desire. Lord keep me from all sin for evermore, that my heart may surely there be fixed; where only true joy is to be found through Jesus Christ my saviour and redeemer. Amen. Seek the Lord forever. Amen.

On 31 August 1837, Thomas Bates was executed for the wilful murder of James Giltrow. He was hanged publicly outside Aylesbury Town Hall in front of a small crowd. At this time, the general public was growing weary of public hangings and only really attended the more sensational executions.

Following Bates' execution, a pamphlet was produced containing extracts from letters he had written. These were distributed to other prisoners presumably as some form of deterrent, but also to journalists for publication and so presumably again for the purpose of deterring would-be criminals from acting on their violent impulses.

CASE TWO 1845

'GIVE, AND IT SHALL BE GIVEN TO YOU'

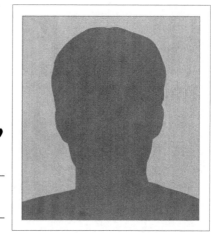

Slough

Suspect:	John Tawell
Age:	61
Charge:	Murder

New Years' Day 1845 should have heralded a new year of hope amid the festive celebrations enjoyed countrywide, but for Sarah Hart (*née* Laurence) aged thirty-nine, it was the last day she would spend on earth. Her body was discovered at Bath Place in Salt Hill, and so began one of the most infamous murder cases in British history.

John Tawell, sixty-one and a resident of London, had been a regular visitor to Sarah Hart. On the day of the murder, he travelled from London to Salt Hill to pay Hart some money he owed.

Tawell was seen leaving Hart's house before he fled back to London by train via Slough station. Sarah Hart's moribund body was discovered almost immediately. This provided the police with the opportunity to track down the suspect before he had time to make his getaway. However, upon arrival at Slough station, the train for Paddington had just departed and the suspect would now have time to divest himself of any incriminating evidence and to potentially arrange an alibi. They needed to communicate with Paddington station in order to prevent the suspect from escaping, but how was this to be done in 1845?

The electric telegraph had not long been invented but a message was sent from Slough to Paddington station telling them to arrest the 'man in the Quaker garb'. The message arrived in time and John Tawell

Salt Hill, where Sarah Hart lived. Bath Place no longer exists. (Author's collection)

was arrested for the murder of Sarah Hart, in the process becoming the first murderer caught by electric telegraph (Dr Crippen was the first man to be captured by the wireless telegraph some sixty-five years later). The message was initially misinterpreted as the telegraph machines did not contain the full twenty-six letters of the alphabet, Q being one of the absent consonants.

It appears Tawell had once lived with Hart and she had claimed that they were married, but this appears to have been a hope rather than a fact. She had two children and it was generally assumed that Tawell was the father. He had visited her throughout the duration of her pregnancies, moving her to various lodgings in search of an element of privacy. Tawell tired of her and moved her to a house in Slough which he hoped would afford them greater privacy while he took up with a respectable Quaker lady in London. Tawell had been married to another woman before he lived with Hart, but his wife died leaving him free to pursue his new paramour. Hart told all her neighbours she had once been in Tawell's employ as a servant but they had married. His absence was explained by the falsehood that he was working abroad for five years.

Slough station, where John Tawell made his escape back to London (Ben Brooksbank, www.geograph.org.uk)

Fearing for his respectability and social standing, he decided Hart was an embarrassment so he set out to do away with her. He visited her on New Years' Day to take her some money, which was not unusual, but he also took with him a phial of prussic acid with which he would murder the unfortunate woman. As Hart struggled for life, Tawell departed for London. He may have escaped had it not been for the suspicions of a neighbour who raised the alarm. Tragically for Hart, her neighbour was unable to save her but her swift action meant the suspected killer was apprehended on his return to London.

'a phial of prussic acid'

This method of murder was not uncommon in the Victorian era but could be particularly cruel if a small but lethal dose was administered. Prussic acid, or hydrogen cyanide as it is now widely known, is a common component of rat poison and chemical weapons. A development of hydrogen cyanide, called zyklon B, was used by the Nazis almost 100 years later in their extermination of the Jews at numerous death camps in mainland Europe.

Death is usually fairly swift, with the victim overcome by the poison soon after ingesting it, often in a faint or a coma until death arrives minutes later. Of course, the speed at which the poison acts would depend on the dose. Poor Sarah Hart endured an agonising death as the effects of the poison took several minutes before death relieved her suffering.

The coroner's inquest commenced the next day, Thursday, 2 January 1845, before Coroner John Charsley. The inquest was adjourned twice, such was the detail the jury was subjected to. Mary Ann Ashlee, who lived next door to Sarah Hart, told how she saw the accused arrive at Hart's between four and five in the afternoon. Between six and seven o'clock that evening she heard muffled screams emanating from Hart's house that lasted for over a minute. Concerned for her neighbour's well-being, Ashlee took a candle and went to Hart's home. As she approached, she saw a man dressed as a Quaker leaving hurriedly and in an agitated state. He could not unlock the gate so she helped and in doing so, saw his face by the light of her candle. Ashlee asked the man what was wrong with Hart but he made no reply and continued on his way. It was the same man she had seen arrive at the house two hours earlier. Alarmed by the events unfolding before her, she decided to look in on her neighbour. She found Hart on the floor, apparently fresh from a struggle. She was gasping for breath and continued making the same muffled screams. Ashlee locked the door after her as she was concerned the fleeing man may return, after he had paused to watch her enter the house.

Hart was in a very distressed state and was unable to speak so Ashlee alerted the neighbours and returned to Hart's side with Mary Jane Barrett, who lived in one of the other houses which formed the row of terraced houses. They attempted to comfort the distressed woman, who, by now, was exuding a muttering cry as her condition worsened. A lad was despatched to request the attendance of a surgeon, Henry Montagu Champneys. When she was raised up from the floor, Hart began to froth at the mouth. Those present also noticed some froth on the table next to a glass.

Earlier that day Hart had told Ashlee that she expected Tawell to visit her to bring her some money. Another witness, Kesiah Harding, who worked for Sarah Hart by way of cleaning her laundry, said she had seen Tawell several times and he had always visited dressed in the attire of a Quaker. Harding saw

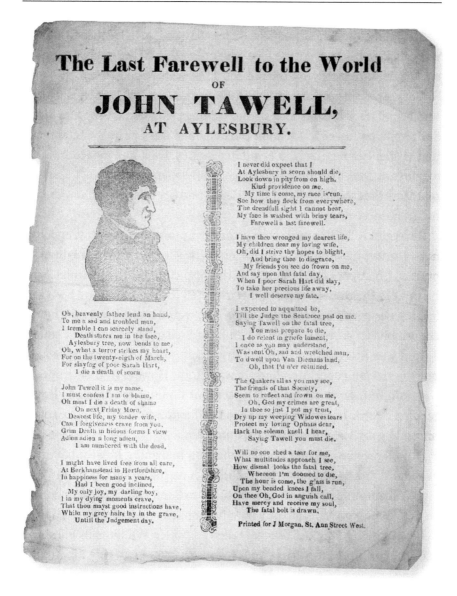

Broadsheet showing an artist's impression of John Tawell. (Courtesy of Douglas Stewart Fine Books)

Tawell at the house in Bath Place a week before the murder when he brought Hart some money. Hart told her, after Tawell had left, that he had only brought a sovereign but she had expected thirteen. Tawell told her he would return in a week with the rest of the money.

At this juncture, Tawell was brought into the court to be identified. Once this was completed, he was escorted out with orders that he be searched as he had not long been in custody and this procedure had yet to be undertaken.

Mary Ann Moss gave her deposition next. Moss had known Hart for a number of years having once shared lodgings with her at Crawford Street. She identified Tawell as the man Hart claimed was her husband and who had visited her regularly to bring her money. Hart had moved from the lodgings as Tawell wanted her to reside somewhere more private. Hart had told Moss that she left behind sick friends and her relations whom she had not seen since.

Reverend E.T. Champnes, the vicar for Upton-cum-Chalvey, appeared next. He gave his account of the events as he saw them on the night of the murder. Champnes had been told of the suspicious death of Sarah Hart so he went to the railway station. He suspected the man who had been seen leaving the premises dressed as a Quaker, would make his escape by rail. His estimation proved correct. When he arrived at Slough railway station, Tawell was just passing through the ticket office so Champnes sought out the station superintendent, Edward John Howell. In the meantime, the train had departed for Paddington but Champnes witnessed Howell send an electric telegraph message to Paddington to alert the police of the impending arrival of the suspected murderer.

Howell received a reply from Paddington informing him that Sergeant William Williams was following the suspect on the omnibus bound for the city. Williams told how he followed Tawell to Bank and from there he went to the Wellington Monument where he stopped and looked around to see if he was being followed. Tawell failed to notice Williams in pursuit of him but continued to visit various locations before entering Mr Hughes' lodging house at 7 Scott's Yard. Williams waited outside for thirty minutes to see if Tawell moved on again but when he did not, he reported his observations to Howell.

The next morning Howell ordered Williams to apprehend the suspect and take him into custody. Williams, accompanied by Inspector Wiggins, found Tawell in the Jerusalem Coffee Shop – a venue he had visited on his way to the lodging house. Around one o'clock on 2 January 1845, John Tawell was arrested in London. Williams asked Tawell if he had been

The Wellington Monument, Bank, where John Tawell fled after murdering Sarah Hart. (Author's collection)

The Bell opposite Scott's Yard, where John Tawell had lodgings. (Author's collection)

in Slough the previous day. Tawell denied being in Slough not suspecting for a moment that he had been followed back to London.

Inspector Wiggins then showed the court the items found on Tawell when he was searched. Among Tawell's possessions was a letter with a Berkhamstead postmark addressed to Tawell from his 'wife' Sarah Hart dated 1 January 1845. Wiggins asked Tawell if he had been in Slough the previous night, again Tawell denied he had saying that he had not left London. Tawell demanded to know why he was being detained and was informed he was suspected of involvement in the death of a woman at Slough. Tawell claimed not to know anyone in Slough.

Tawell was called back into court and told he would be remanded in custody. He demanded to be read any evidence the police had against him but the coroner rejected this request. Tawell then asked if he may be permitted to return home, again the coroner rejected his overtures. Tawell continued to plead for release on pain of his public duties. The coroner reminded Tawell that he was the last person to see the deceased and would remain in custody.

Cannon Street was on the route taken by John Tawell. (Author's collection)

Cowper's Court, where the Jerusalem Coffee House stood. (Author's collection)

The inquest resumed on Saturday 4 January with the evidence of the attending surgeon Henry Champneys. Champneys told how he was asked to attend a dying woman some 200 yards from his own home and so ran to the home of Sarah Hart, whom he knew only by sight. He found Hart on the floor and felt for a pulse. He observed three beats but then Hart appeared to die moments later. Champneys then opened a vein to see if he could ascertain the cause of death. There was a stout bottle and two glasses on the table at the murder scene, so he asked Mrs Ashlee to secure these so they could be tested for the presence of poison. He then departed for Slough station where he observed the accused man departing for Paddington.

Champneys conducted the post-mortem on Sarah Hart's body assisted by another surgeon, Edward Norblad. There was nothing in any of the organs which would have caused the sudden death. They examined the contents of Hart's stomach but could come to no conclusion before they were properly analysed. They tested for four different poisonous substances, one of which was prussic acid which they did not know had been administered to the victim. This test was positive and the cause of death was officially declared as death by poisoning. The poison had most likely been diluted in a liquid with the purpose of avoiding its detection. It was possible prussic acid salts were used which lack the distinctive almond smell of the liquid form.

Mr Norblad gave similar evidence but had a greater knowledge of the effects of prussic acid. He confirmed that prussic acid was responsible for Hart's death. Both the surgeons had noticed its distinctive smell when opening the stomach. Death would take between two seconds and fifteen minutes and there was enough acid present to be the cause of death.

Upon resumption of the inquest four days later, Norblad continued. He had, in the interlude, examined the contents of the bottle of stout and the glasses found at the scene and confiscated by Mr Champneys. Neither the bottle or the glasses contained any trace of poison but one of the glasses, which had some froth on it, had been rinsed out by Mrs Barrett in order to give the dying woman a sip of water. There was also the remnant of a bun found with the stout and glasses; this too was found to be free of any poison.

Montague Chambers had arrived at the inquest as it closed on the Saturday to defend John Tawell. Chambers proved to be an able and experienced counsel. He disputed that any evidence pointed to his client and countered that it pointed to no one in particular for they knew not how the poison had been administered. Chambers asked permission to address the jury in order to impart some observations but the coroner dismissed the request, however, he would allow Chambers to call witnesses in defence of the accused. Chambers declined this invitation so the coroner addressed the jury and asked them to consider the evidence and decide whether or not they thought the accused should be committed for trial.

The room was cleared and in thirty minutes the jury had come to its conclusion. The coroner told the persons present that the jury had found John Tawell guilty of the wilful and premeditated murder of Sarah Hart by poisoning.

Tawell was then despatched to Aylesbury Gaol to await trial, but not before the members of the public who had gathered in and around the small public house voiced their disgust at the prisoner.

A frenzy of investigation into the past of the accused man ensued. Tawell had not grown up a Quaker but had turned to that faith in his teenage years. Initially, he was declined by the society but was later accepted. However, he married a woman who was not of the Quaker faith, contradicting their rules, and was summarily expelled. He soon broke the law through the medium of forgery and was arrested. Tawell conducted his own defence and faced seven years of hard labour. He entreated the judge to sentence him instead to fourteen years in New South Wales to which the judge acceded. After a few years and observation of his good conduct, he was granted his liberty and he set up a successful business in Sydney as a 'druggist'. A number of years later, he returned to England and procured a splendid house in Regent's Park. He met and married his second wife (not Sarah Hart) who ran an upper-class boarding school in Berkhamstead. She was a Quaker but because Tawell had already been expelled from the Society, upon their marriage she too was expelled. They lived a very

St Mary's in Farnham Royal, where Sarah Hart was buried. (Author's collection)

comfortable existence and although ostracised by the Quakers, Tawell was respected by many of them for his scientific knowledge and his benevolence to charitable organisations.

The trial of John Tawell began one month after the murder, on 1 February 1845, before Judge Parke. It caused a sensation in Aylesbury and attracted large crowds to the County Hall. The prosecution was conducted by Messrs Byles and Prendergast with Messrs O'Malley, Kelly and Gunning defending. The defence objected to eighteen jurors before the trial started. Tawell pleaded not guilty to the charge of wilful murder in a loud and confident voice.

The testimony of the witnesses previously given at the coroner's inquest was repeated but further evidence and witnesses were provided. Katherine White, a barmaid and resident of the Windmill public house deposed that Sarah Hart had visited the hostelry around half past six on New Years' Day to purchase a bottle of stout. She also borrowed a corkscrew before returning home ten minutes later. White was able to confirm the time because she

The graveyard of St Mary's. (Author's collection)

looked at the clock when Hart departed. A local gardener named William Marlow observed the deceased on her return from the Windmill which he confirmed was around six thirty. He spoke to Hart asking her why she was running and in such apparent high spirits.

Next called was a waiter known as John Kendall who was working at the Jerusalem Coffee House at Cornhill. Kendall distinctly remembered Tawell from the day of the murder. Tawell arrived at the coffee shop around three o'clock in the afternoon and asked what time they planned to close that evening as he was going to the West End and wanted to leave behind his coat and a parcel for collection later. Kendall told Tawell they would close at eight o'clock but all Tawell had to do was call whenever he returned. He collected his belongings from Kendall that evening around half past nine.

Henry Crapp who was employed by the Great Western Railway Company told the court he recognised the accused as he had sold him a return train ticket on the day of the murder.

A postboy from Slough, George Lewis, then testified that he had known John Tawell for approximately two years and had seen him around seven o'clock on the evening of the murder, running towards Slough away from the direction of Sarah Hart's home at Bath Place. Lewis saw Tawell by the light of a streetlamp and bid him a greeting that Tawell ignored.

An innkeeper from Eton, Robert Roberts, then told the court how the accused climbed on board an omnibus in Slough bound for Eton. The accused alighted at Herschel House which is about 400 yards from Slough station.

Thomas Cooper was called at the beginning of the second day of the trial. He was the consulting chemist who had examined the contents of Sarah Hart's stomach and had declared prussic acid as the toxin responsible for her death. Cooper explained in great detail the tests he conducted to see what poisons, if any, were present in the stomach of the deceased.

Charlotte Howard, an acquaintance of Sarah Hart, delivered testimony that alluded to the accused having attempted the murder, unsuccessfully, once before in September 1844. She had stayed with Hart a number of times and had seen Tawell in her company twice before. Another time, she was staying with Hart for a fortnight when Tawell arrived. Hart asked Howard to obtain a bottle of stout. Shortly afterwards, she asked Howard to collect a sheet of paper from a neighbour. At this time she seemed perfectly well. Again, Howard obliged but on her return Hart had suddenly become quite ill. Hart was sick and developed severe nausea, so much so that she asked her master to go. Hart told Howard she had only drunk one small glass of stout but now felt dreadful. Howard put Hart to bed, where she was sick again, then went to the room where the stout and the glasses were. She threw away the contents of the glasses but drank the stout that remained in the bottle and suffered no ill effects whatsoever.

The defence attempted to cast doubt upon the evidence given by the three surgeons by disputing the effects of prussic poisoning. This was easier in 1845 as they did not have the forensic capabilities we now have. They even called into question the sense of smell of Mr Norblad!

Henry Thomas heaped more fatal evidence upon Tawell when he testified that Tawell had visited the pharmacy where he worked on 1 January 1845, between twelve and two in the afternoon and purchased a quantity of prussic acid. Thomas was labelling the bottle when Tawell told him there was no need; he labelled it anyway. Thomas saw Tawell again the following day, between ten and twelve in the morning, when he returned to purchase more prussic acid. Tawell claimed to have damaged the previous batch through a minor misfortune.

The defence then proceeded to call a number of character witnesses who testified to the accused man's good character. Despite the nature of the crime, the defence were able to call a large number of people to testify.

The closing speeches were delivered and the judge adjourned the court until the following morning.

Friday morning saw the court packed again and the judge sum up the pertinent facts to the jury. He instructed them to ignore the sensationalism surrounding the trial and any rumour or report they had heard. They must deliver their verdict on the facts as they had heard them in the courtroom. The decision of the jury rested on who they believed administered the prussic acid. Tawell claimed Sarah Hart had taken it of her own free will. The prosecution alleged that it was given to her without her knowledge by Tawell. After the judge's summing up, which lasted four hours, the jury retired to consider their verdict. They deliberated for just half an hour before returning a guilty verdict for the wilful murder of Sarah Hart.

The judge placed the black cap on his head and passed a sentence of death upon John Tawell. Tawell looked greatly affected by the pronouncement but said nothing in response and was escorted from the dock.

As the execution approached, Tawell indulged in writing prolifically. His appearance suffered from the stress of the certain future he now faced and he expressed a wish to get it over with as soon as possible.

On the eve of the execution the chaplain and the prison governor spent the entire night with the condemned man. Tawell spent most of the time praying, occasionally resorting to tears and obvious signs of repentance. He retired to his bed around four with a request to be woken an hour later. He woke before the hour expired and asked to be served his refreshments, which he invited the governor and chaplain to share with him. He had finally written a confession but did not offer it to the attendants, choosing to keep it in his pocket instead. At regular intervals he would produce the document, read it through and return it to his pocket. The governor reminded him that he was expected to sign a confession before the appointed time. Eventually Tawell offered the confession to the chaplain.

Tawell confirmed the accusations made in court were an accurate appraisal of the events leading to the death of Sarah Hart. He admitted that he had attempted to kill Hart the first time in September 1844, when he had administered poison to her stout. On this occasion he did not use prussic acid. Tawell claimed his motive had not been malice towards Hart but one of fear of his wife discovering their relationship. He did not begrudge her the money he paid as it did not amount to much. He was unaware Hart had told anyone in Slough of his existence and presumed he would be able to slip back into London unnoticed.

John Tawell was publicly executed outside the County Hall in Aylesbury on 28 March 1845. Crowds started to gather from six o'clock in the morning with people walking from the villages surrounding Aylesbury and by seven there was in excess of 3,000 people awaiting Tawell's gruesome demise. By eight o'clock, the time of the execution, there were around 6,000 people gathered.

Shortly before the appointed time, Tawell mounted the scaffold and was pinioned. He was granted permission to pray and he fell to his knees in pious communication for a minute or two before the procedure commenced.

Broadsheet for the execution of John Tawell. (Courtesy of Douglas Stewart Fine Books)

The hood was placed over his head by William Calcraft, the executioner, who then made the final adjustments. While Tawell continued to pray, the bolt was removed and he dropped to his doom. Fortune did not smile on Tawell for unlike many who were hanged, he did not die swiftly. He struggled and convulsed for a number of minutes before he ceased all movement. The strong winds then swung his lifeless body back and forth; an hour later he was cut down and an hour after that he was buried in an unmarked grave within the precincts of Aylesbury Gaol.

Broadsheet reporting Tawell's life story. (Courtesy of Douglas Stewart Fine Books)

CASE THREE 1864

'OH DEATH WHERE IS THY STING?'

Buckingham

Suspect:	William Stevens
Age:	24
Charge:	Murder

The 27 February 1864, saw a sensation in the attractive town of Buckingham and the surrounding areas. A man named William John Stevens had killed a woman named Annie Leeson and then attempted to take his own life.

The murderer and victim lived next door to each other on Nelson Street. Twenty-four-year-old Stevens was a tailor, like his father, and lived with his parents. His father, Robert was reputed to be a 'remarkably sober, steady and quiet man'. Annie Leeson was just seventeen years old and the youngest daughter of an aging widow. Leeson did not spend much time at her family home as she was employed by a relative, James Uff, as a domestic a few doors further down the street in his home and shop.

It was reported that Robert Stevens' late employer, Mr Ladd, had retained high hopes for Stevens becoming a highly talented tailor, describing him as having the admirable personality of his father. However, after serving his apprenticeship under the tutelage of Mr Ladd, William Stevens travelled to London where he remained for two years mixing with dubious company and developing socially unacceptable habits.

On his return to Buckingham, Stevens became besotted with Leeson but she did not reciprocate and made no secret of this. He sent her two expensive gifts for Valentine's Day but these did not enamour him to her.

Nelson Street: Annie Leeson lived on the left and William Stevens on the right. (Author's collection)

Stevens displayed jealousy when she conversed with other young men, but it was her natural disposition to be friendly and smiling.

This would induce a rage in Stevens which eventually manifested itself with the vicious murder of the young woman. Stevens had boasted several times that he would cut Leeson's throat but those who heard this 'chest thumping' ascribed it to attempted intimidation so that Leeson would receive his romantic overtures. Stevens' father found his son had taken to carrying a razor with him and immediately confiscated it. However, Stevens managed to retrieve the razor and it was with this that he brutally murdered the object of his desires. Sadly, no one had taken Stevens seriously, hence poor Annie Leeson continued as normal with no knowledge of the impending threats that hung over her.

Around six o'clock in the evening, Stevens had returned home from work. He was upstairs dressing himself when he saw Leeson pass the house carrying a bucket to collect some

Mr Uff's grocery and general store – Annie Leeson's place of work. (Author's collection)

water from the nearby pump at Hunter Street. Stevens waited for her return then ran outside after her. Leeson was outside Mrs Spicer's further along Nelson Street when, from behind, Stevens drew the razor across her throat. He delivered a second slash moments later and Leeson dropped the bucket. Despite the horrific attack and mortal injuries she sustained, Leeson managed to retain her balance and continued to Mr Uff's shop, some 20 yards further along Nelson Street. Her throat was gushing blood

'Her throat was gushing blood'

all the way and upon entering Uff's shop she went towards him, her arms extended in a silent plea for help. Uff caught the girl and she looked at him as if to speak but no sound was forthcoming. Uff could see the horrific wound; her head was almost severed from her body. He removed her at once to his house where he held a cloth to her throat in a vain attempt to

The water pump at the junction of Hunter Street and Nelson Street. (Author's collection)

stem the profuse bleeding. James Uff sat on a chair with the dying girl's head rested upon him. She made no sound except the occasional sigh and within a minute she breathed no more.

Police Constable Seaton was in Uff's butchery and grocery shop, which adjoined his house, when the hapless girl burst in. He saw the extent of the injuries and immediately set off to seek medical assistance. The somewhat aptly, if macabre sounding, Dr Death soon arrived astride his grand black horse from his home a few streets away. It was too late, Annie Leeson was dead. Dr Robert Death was then called to the Stevens' home. Following the attack on Leeson, William Stevens had twice tried to slash his own throat with the same razor with which he had murdered his victim. His mother witnessed this and prevented him inflicting a third and potentially fatal wound; although for some time it was considered Stevens would not recover from the injuries. Dr Death stitched the wounds and Stevens survived to face justice for his selfish and violent actions. He was arrested and charged

Mrs Spicer's house, outside which the murder was committed. (Author's collection)

with wilful murder. Annie Leeson's mother also witnessed Stevens' suicide attempts and sought out her daughter to tell her what had happened. It was only then that she discovered Leeson's fate, finding her daughter in the final agonising moments of her life in Uff's shop.

Mr Uff and his family suffered terribly as a result of the crime and became quite ill after having witnessed such a horrific scene. Stevens appeared to show remorse and only wished to be allowed to die and be buried next to his brother. Alas for Stevens, convicted murderers are buried in unconsecrated ground in accordance with the law and have no choice where that may be.

Once arrested, he was guarded in his bed for five weeks while he recovered and then conveyed to Buckingham Gaol, where he remained until he was transferred to Aylesbury. Stevens was guarded constantly by a policeman and two nurses to ensure he could not harm himself while in custody, enabling the law to take its full and natural course. He regularly asked to be left alone so he might save them the bother of watching him. He refused to take food and was

Hamilton House, where Dr Death lived. (Author's collection)

content to pass from this life to the next at the soonest opportunity. He would only accept water and this would seep out of the self-inflicted wounds he had sustained on his throat. It was considered he would not survive long from his hunger strike in his weakened state.

The coroner's inquest opened on Monday 29 February at the Red Lion Inn (near Mr Uff's house) before Coroner D.P. King. The jury of sixteen men was sworn in, led by the foreman Mr H. Sanders. Their first duty was to visit Mr Uff's house where Leeson's body lay in order to inspect the corpse. They then returned to the Red Lion to hear evidence concerning the circumstances surrounding her death.

James Uff was the first called and he cut a sorry figure. He retold the events of the murder as he had witnessed them. He confirmed he had heard Stevens boast of how he would kill Leeson but that she had not been frightened so no one else had taken the threats seriously.

Next to give evidence was one of Leeson's older sisters, Elizabeth. She told the inquest that Leeson had walked with Stevens on a number of occasions

Buckingham Gaol, where William Stevens was held. (Author's collection)

The former Red Lion, where the inquest was held. (Author's collection)

but that the last time they had walked together, just over a week before the murder took place, Leeson had returned in a temper. She complained that Stevens had behaved inappropriately to her and that she swore never to walk with him again.

Leeson went to visit another sister in Well Street on the Thursday before she was murdered and asked Elizabeth to accompany her. Elizabeth could not escort her sister that evening and it transpired that Stevens was waiting and followed Leeson to her sister's house, where he waited outside for her.

Elizabeth described how on the day of the murder she saw her sister around six o'clock in the evening when Leeson entered the family home where Elizabeth was alone. They heard Stevens walk down the passage and go into his kitchen. Assuming she could leave unhindered, Leeson said, 'Lizzie, he's gone down the yard and I'll go.' But when Leeson left, Stevens emerged from his kitchen and followed her up the passage towards the street. Elizabeth heard the sound of a tussle or of a person falling and went out to the passage to investigate. Mrs Stevens, William's mother,

The passageway separating the homes of Annie Leeson and William Stevens. (Author's collection)

The yard where William Stevens was found after slashing his own throat. (Author's collection)

did likewise and brought with her a candle to illuminate the dingy passageway. They found William Stevens on the ground with fresh blood splattered all around. Confronted with this macabre tableau, Elizabeth fled and returned to her home.

Elizabeth also recalled how Leeson had told her that Stevens had shown her the razor but did not know if he made direct threats to her about using it. Stevens did threaten Leeson, saying that if she were to marry anyone else he would blow her brains out.

There was an independent witness to the murder, a thirteen-year-old boy by the name of Richard Woolhead. He saw the attack and the events leading up to it and retold his observations to the inquest. Woolhead saw Annie Leeson at the water pump at the old churchyard corner where she filled her bucket and then set off in the direction of her mother's house. Here she stopped for a few minutes before heading towards Mr Uff's house and shop. William Stevens emerged from his house and followed closely behind Leeson but she did not look around to see who it was. Woolhead

The old churchyard corner, where Richard Woolhead witnessed the murder. (Author's collection)

saw Stevens grab Leeson from behind and reach around, dragging something across her throat. Stevens ran off and Woolhead heard Leeson simply say one word – murder.

A tailor from Buckingham called John Billing who, like Stevens, was in the employ of Mrs Ladd, told how he and the accused had been drinking in the Barrel public house when Stevens told him he would kill Leeson if it wasn't for the law. He even declared his motive – jealousy.

Billing saw Stevens after the murder, as did a foundry man called George Finch. Both said Stevens knew that he had committed a heinous deed and appeared truly repentant for his actions. Additionally, he regretted being unable to finish himself off afterwards.

The surgeon Dr Death then gave his testimony. He had been called to attend Annie Leeson but was stopped enroute as she was, by this time, already dead. Instead he was diverted to William Stevens who was expected to die shortly. After some pretty miraculous work on Stevens, Dr Death went to see the body of Annie Leeson. He described her wounds thus: 'There was a large wound in the throat extending from about half an inch below the right ear across the middle of the throat to about an inch below the left ear. The windpipe and gullet were cut through as also the vessels of the neck.'

He continued, 'I have no doubt the cause of death was the bleeding from the wound in the throat.'

The evidence was clear and indisputable with the jury taking just five minutes to agree the accused be charged with wilful murder.

Annie Leeson's body was buried on Tuesday, 1 March 1864, by the Revd Humphries. The murder garnered interest from the local communities, who raised a public subscription in excess of £10 to help the family with the costs of burying the young girl. The jury at the inquest generously donated their fees to the fund.

On 18 July 1864 the trial commenced before Baron Martin, in Aylesbury, with a full and frantic courtroom. It was initially intended to try Stevens at the Spring Assizes but he had not sufficiently recovered from his injuries at that time, so his trial was postponed until the Midsummer Assizes. The case

The graveyard where Annie Leeson was buried. (Author's collection)

provided sensational headlines, encouraging those in the locale to attend in large numbers. Order was maintained but only after some considerable effort by those assisting the officials in their duties.

The accused was brought to the dock looking pale and unwell. Bereft of any substance of height or build, Stevens portrayed a sorry sight. He wore a blue neckerchief to conceal the self-inflicted wounds and was provided with a seat in consideration of his physical condition.

In a firm but hushed voice, William Stevens pleaded not guilty to the charge of wilful murder. He cannot have expected anything other than a guilty verdict but retained the remote hope that he could evade the hangman's noose, of which he had a loathsome abhorrence. Stevens did not fear the penalty of death for his crime, more he dreaded the method by which he would be dispatched if found guilty.

The jury, with Daniel Clare assuming the responsibility of foreman, was sworn in without Stevens objecting to any of its members. Messrs Keane and Markby appeared for the prosecution with Mr Payne appointed to defend the prisoner.

As custom dictated, the prosecution began with the opening speech. Mr Keane QC recited the events but also added that there was no provocation on the part of the victim and therefore, no leniency could be sought by the accused. Stevens, Keane confidently asserted, had acted upon a jealous impulse and was perfectly aware of his actions as he had previously described his intentions to sceptical work colleagues.

Thirteen-year-old Richard Woolhead gave his testimony first. There was some question over whether he was a fit witness, due to his age and lack of education (he was illiterate), but when questioned about whether or not he could tell lies in court, the young lad told the court if he did he would expect to go to gaol.

The witnesses from the coroner's inquest then recalled their evidence before the court. Elizabeth, Annie Leeson's sister who had discovered Stevens in the passageway attempting to end his own life, was dressed in her mourning garb. She was quite overcome by the affair and had to be seated and aroused with smelling salts. She recovered enough to deliver her testimony in hushed tones. Midway through, Elizabeth fainted and had to be revived to continue her deposition. The judge consoled the tragic sister of the victim, asking her not to be afraid of the man in the dock who stared at her intently and to deliver her evidence in a calm manner. Elizabeth was not the only witness overcome by the occasion. John Billing, who had worked with Stevens, gave his evidence in such a whispered fashion the judge threatened to dismiss his evidence unless he spoke more loudly and behaved not 'so silly'.

Police Superintendent William Giles was called to give his evidence. Mr Payne – defending – attempted to discredit his evidence, asserting that Giles had not cautioned the prisoner and subsequently anything he said could not be given in evidence against him. Giles agreed that he had not cautioned Stevens but he had not, at any time, asked the prisoner any questions. The evidence he gave was a recollection of a statement made by the accused entirely of his own volition. As no questioning or inducement to talk was made and the identity of the superintendent was known to the prisoner, he felt it had been unnecessary to caution him.

Giles told the court that Stevens had said to him:

Oh Mr Giles, that scaffold at Aylesbury. Am I to be buried in a prison? To die there and be buried in the gaol yard and be covered up with hot lime, I cannot. Let me die on the bed as I am. I wish Dr Death had been out at the time and then I should have been dead and I should now have been in heaven with my dear Annie.

Stevens continued, 'How could I do it? How could I do it? Bit I did it.' This caused great excitement in the courtroom.

Police Constable Humphrey Ray identified a razor produced in court as the one he recovered from the prisoner's mother on the evening of the murder. It was soaked with blood. Ray was one of the policemen who kept a vigil over the accused to ensure he did not harm himself further while in custody. He heard Stevens repeatedly ask, 'How could I do it?' Stevens was also alleged to say, 'I wish she was alive and I was dead.' Illuminating Stevens' motive further, Ray deposed that Mr Finch asked Stevens why he did it. Stevens replied, 'Against Mrs Spicer's I spoke as civil to her as a man could speak but she would not speak to me but swung about and then I did it.'

Another policeman who had kept a watchful eye over the prisoner in the days after the murder, recounted how Stevens had told him if Leeson had simply bid 'good night' as he did to her, he should not have committed the terrible deed. Stevens made a fuller confession: 'I caught her on Mrs Spicer's doorstep and there I did it. After I did it I did not know where to run. I then ran back to my own door and cut my throat twice and tried a third time but I fell.'

The case for the prosecution was settled. The weight of evidence was insurmountable. Stevens remained unemotional during the proceedings except during James Uff's evidence concerning Leeson's death, when he betrayed signs of deep emotion.

Mr Payne then delivered a lengthy and impassioned plea for the defence. The evidence against the accused appeared to be indisputable yet Payne's closing speech was robust, intelligent and credible. Payne alluded to the weight of evidence, observing that his client had indeed killed Annie Leeson. Payne asserted that the crime was not a result of malice afore-thought or of lengthy planning but one of frenzied momentary insanity. Why would a man destroy the object of his affections for then he could never have her for himself? The motive was flimsy. Therefore, the defence asked that a charge of manslaughter be considered.

Payne dissected the testimony of the thirteen-year-old Richard Woolhead. Woolhead was the only witness to the crime but he was young, had never attended school, could not read or write and was therefore, an unreliable witness. This was especially pertinent as the life of a man was dependent on the testimony given by a child. Of course, in reality there is no reason to suppose a thirteen-year-old could not provide reliable testimony, but Payne's duty was to implant doubt in the minds of the jurors. He also highlighted the point that none of Woolhead's evidence had been or could be corroborated.

He was not finished; Payne then deconstructed the evidence provided by the police. The surgeon Dr Death had deposed that Stevens was at death's door and yet the police questioned Stevens recovering in his bed the following morning without even cautioning him. The statements of the police, therefore, ought to be discarded as Stevens was in no fit state to provide an accurate account of the events of the day before.

Stevens clearly loved Annie Leeson so why should he kill her? If the jury accepted Stevens was responsible for the wounds that took her life they had to consider whether Stevens had planned the attack in advance, or if it had been a reaction to an event that occurred between them immediately before the murder. The difference, Payne asserted, was that between wilful murder and manslaughter. The only person alive who knew what had gone between killer and victim was the accused and he was not at liberty to give evidence at his own trial.

Payne concluded by asking the jury to examine their consciences and should they believe without any doubt that murder had indeed been committed, they should display their consideration of the circumstances in which it was conducted and recommend the judge to mercy. This induced a swift rebuke from the judge who told him it would never be done, but the able Payne replied, citing a legal precedent from a recent case.

The judge summed up and told the jury they should not return a verdict of manslaughter for no man had the right to destroy a woman simply for denying his advances. The jury's decision was simple; the wounds inflicted by the assailant were responsible for her death, therefore the person who inflicted those wounds was guilty of murder. Had William Stevens inflicted those wounds? If the jury accepted he had then they must return a guilty verdict.

The jury retired for thirteen minutes before the foreman, Mr Sanders, in an emotional and quiet voice returned a verdict of guilty of wilful murder. Stevens was given the opportunity to speak but he said nothing, staring with an empty gaze already resigned to his fate. In accordance with procedure, the judge put on the black cap and announced a sentence of death.

The last public execution in Aylesbury was conducted outside Aylesbury Gaol in the archway entrance, on 5 August 1864. Before he met his fate, Stevens met briefly with his family.

Crowds had been gathering from five o'clock in the morning the day before the execution was due, in order to procure a vantage point from which to observe the hanging of William Stevens. It was claimed that the scene could be watched from much further afield with a decent pair of field glasses, which many attempted such was the excitement generated by this tragic affair. The execution was due to commence at eight o'clock

The front gate at Aylesbury Gaol, where William Stevens was hanged.
(Author's collection)

in the morning and shortly before, a crowd numbering around 4,000 had congregated around the gaol. Around forty policemen, some on horseback, were employed to maintain order for it was feared the crowd would surge forward in order to gain an improved view of the event but the crowd, made up of the middle and working classes, behaved impeccably.

The bell of the parish church chimed shortly before the appointed time and a most solemn but sincere outlook was adopted by those gathered. The executioner, William Calcraft, checked the scaffold and then disappeared again to fetch the prisoner from his cell. The order of execution was read aloud while the prisoner remained immoveable in silent meditation. He only then turned to the chaplain to express his penitence and wish for forgiveness in the next world. He then mounted the scaffold, but fainted as he reached the final step and gained a full view of the apparatus of death awaiting him. Fortunately, he was caught by the warder and quickly recovered. The crowd watched, almost in silence, the occasional comment clearly audible in the eerie hush.

The rope was placed over Stevens' neck and he pleaded loudly for God to help him. A white hood was then placed over his head and he again pleaded with God for assistance in his final moments. The silence was then shattered by the trapdoor opening, the clank of the chain to which the noose was attached and the thud of Stevens' body plummeting through the drop. The crowd, as one, released a gasp but it appeared death was not instantaneous as the body writhed and struggled for almost five minutes before finally becoming still.

The crowds dispersed, with a few hundred waiting the full hour for the body of the condemned man to be cut down.

Many rumours, mostly inaccurate and ridiculously sensational, circulated so on the day of the execution the gaol released a statement:

The prisoner, ever since his conviction, has conducted himself in the most satisfactory manner and the chaplain (Revd Rawson) of the prison speaks of him as having been most attentive to his ministrations and very earnest in his preparation for death. He has never since his sentence denied his guilt or attempted to palliate his crime and he has fully acknowledged the justice of his sentence. He met his fate with resignation and fortitude and his last moments were spent in prayer and supplication for God's help.

It is said that Annie Leeson's house is haunted by her ghost, however, the current occupant has made friends with her and they live together peacefully.

CASE FOUR 1870

'FEAR NOT THEM WHICH KILL THE BODY'

Little Linford

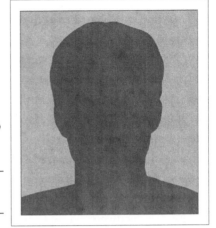

Suspect:	William Mobbs
Age:	20
Charge:	Murder

On Thursday, 22 July 1869, in the sleepy Buckinghamshire village of Little Linford, William Mobbs was working for William Payne, a farm tenant, keeping birds from his cornfields. William Scott who owned the adjacent farm employed James Newbury and his two sons in a similar capacity. James' son Thomas, who was just ten years old, was working that day and went across to see William Mobbs. Mobbs, aged twenty, had promised to give Newbury a percussion cap for a pistol if he saw him. It was the last time Thomas was seen alive.

At around six o'clock that evening, a labourer from Hanslope by the name of Joseph Staunton, who also worked for Mr Scott, was returning home along an occupation road (freeboard) that separated the two farms when he made a gruesome discovery. Beside a hedge in a pea field he found the dead and bloodied body of a ten-year-old boy, later identified as Thomas James Newbury. The body lay in a pool of blood, which was caused by the young victim's throat being cut so deeply his head was almost separated from his body.

Staunton immediately requested assistance from those in the locale and the police in Newport Pagnell were sent for. Tragically, the poor boy's father was one of the first people to arrive at the horrific scene.

Inspector Hall received information that the boy had gone to see William Mobbs to procure the percussion cap for a pistol and since then

Mobbs had been seen, but had discarded some of his clothing. Inspector Hall visited the house belonging to Mobbs' father in Marsh End, Newport Pagnell, and found the suspect utterly naked in bed. After a search of the premises, he located Mobbs' shirt, which was covered in blood on the

'The body lay in a pool of blood'

lower ends of the sleeves. Hall also recovered further clothing that was splattered with blood.

Mobbs attempted to escape suspicion by producing a bloodless brown smock and declaring he had worn it at work that day. However, this claim was disputed by those who had seen him at work and disputed further when it became known that the brown smock actually belonged to his brother. Mobbs was arrested and taken into custody.

A search of the site of the murder was conducted shortly afterwards and a knife was found by James Newbury, the murdered boy's father.

The fields where William Mobbs and Thomas Newbury toiled. (Author's collection)

The knife was identified, by a number of people present, as belonging to Mobbs. Inspector Hall and Mr Scott (the tenant farmer) also found a discarded white slop (loose outer garment like a smock) in a hedge about 90 yards from where the dead boy had been found. It was covered in blood and witnesses confirmed that it was the one Mobbs had been wearing that day at work in the fields. The discovery of the slop was due to the astute detective work of Inspector Hall. He noticed a slight flattening of grass just off the occupation road that led to a small wood, so, following the way, he found the slop hanging on some bushes where it could not be seen from the occupation road.

There was no apparent motive for the crime so many wild theories circulated. *The Bucks Herald* printed one theory, which they correctly considered was nothing more than village gossip. It was reported that Mobbs and Newbury had raided a pigeon's nest and had each a

St Mary's church, Haversham, where Thomas Newbury was buried. (Author's collection)

The graveyard at St Mary's church. (Author's collection)

young pigeon. Mobbs coveted Newbury's pigeon and in an argument the fatal deed was committed.

The coroner's inquest on the boy's body took place at his parents' cottage in Haversham the next day, Friday, 23 July 1869, conducted by J. Worley, with the jury led by Henry Pike of Haversham.

The tragic sight of James Newbury greeted the jury, honour-bound as he was to give evidence less than twenty-four hours after he had seen the savaged body of his young son. Newbury simply recounted his knowledge of his son's final day on earth and the events that happened after the body was discovered.

The surgeon who inspected the body at the murder site the evening before, William Rogers of Wolverton, described the injuries inflicted upon James Newbury and the circumstances surrounding his death as he perceived them. These would prove a contentious issue later at the trial:

I examined the body and found several incised wounds on the throat, from four to four and-a-half inches in length, dividing the principal arteries and the windpipe. They were not clean cuts and were made from left to right. There was also a wound on the side of the neck about half or three quarters of an inch in length from the commencement and about an inch in depth. The knife produced would be likely to produce such wounds and death must have been almost instantaneous. The body had been dragged from one place to another and there were traces of blood on the grass over where the body had been dragged. The grass was smeared over with blood. It is impossible that the wounds could have been inflicted by the deceased himself. I have also examined the whole of the body externally. There is a slight wound on the centre of the forehead and there are also slight bruises on the on both legs. There is also a slight scratch on the hand but evidently not done with a knife. The body was rigid and there were a number of fly-blows on the wounds and on the side of the face. Life had been extinct about three hours or more when I saw the body. The features were placid. I have examined the spot where the body was found and there appears to have been two places where the body had been lying – one close to the hedge and the other about ten yards into the field. There were two pools of blood, one of them where the body was found being about one-and-a-half yards from the hedge. The body had evidently been dragged from one place to the other. There was a slight trail of blood smeared over the grass.

The inquest was adjourned until Monday and, thankfully, it was resumed at the National Schoolroom instead of the home of the deceased. A schoolroom may appear to be an unusual venue but buildings suitable for coping with the number of people at an inquest were not freely available, especially in smaller villages.

A labourer from Haversham named John Morris deposed that on the day of the murder he had seen the victim, Thomas Newbury, at around two o'clock. They were working in adjacent fields and Newbury had visited him for a drink of water. He left around thirty minutes later, saying that he had to go and see Mobbs at three o'clock because Mobbs had promised to give him a percussion cap. Morris did not see the boy again until the alarm was raised by Mr Staunton later that day. He recognised the murdered boy and located his father to inform him of the tragic news.

Inspector Hall told the court that he took possession of Thomas Newbury's effects, including his blood drenched clothing, on the evening he was murdered. In a pocket of the boy's trousers he found a copper percussion cap. It had been the promise of the percussion cap that had lured Newbury to his untimely demise. He also retold finding the discarded slop which was obscured from the view of passers-by.

Hall continued; when he apprehended Mobbs at his father's home at Marsh End, he took possession of Mobbs' clothing. Amongst his belongings, he found some copper percussion caps that exactly matched the one found in the pocket of the victim. The sleeves of the shirt Mobbs had been wearing that day were rolled up so Inspector Hall started to unroll them. Mobbs declared 'you will find nothing there' but Hall found blood on both wrist-bands. Mobbs dismissed this as a result of a nosebleed. Hall found blood on the accused's trousers and his belt but Mobbs offered no explanation for this. When arrested Mobbs simply exclaimed 'Me!' His mother asked him if he had seen Thomas Newbury and Mobbs replied that he had but not since eleven o'clock.

Thomas Coaley, a labourer from Stoke Goldington, delivered a very illu-minating testimony. He had been ploughing with Mobbs on the morning of the murder after the boy he had been working with previously went to fetch some beer. He had noticed Mobbs was wearing a white slop. He identified it by a brown patch and a hole it bore and confirmed the one produced in evidence was the one Mobbs had been wearing on the day of the murder. He refuted Mobbs' claim to Inspector Hall that he had been wearing a brown smock on the day of the murder and went on to state that he had never seen Mobbs in such a garment but that he had seen Mobbs' brother wearing it. Coaley left Mobbs around two o'clock to move to a lower field to mow thistles. He next saw Mobbs around half-past four and by this time Mobbs had discarded his white slop and rolled his shirtsleeves up to the elbow. He was carrying with him his pistol, which he used to scare birds from the fields as part of his work. Mobbs asked Coaley if he had seen Bill Bates, to which Coaley replied he had just seen him go through the gate. Coaley asked Mobbs what time it was but Mobbs refused to tell him, citing the hurry he was in as the reason why. Coaley also identified the murder weapon as belonging to Mobbs as he had borrowed it himself only the Tuesday before to cut a stick.

Coaley said that he did not know Thomas Newbury and did not recall ever seeing him, but he did have to step in about three weeks earlier when Mobbs was bullying a different boy. Coaley had told Mobbs that if he wanted to push someone around he should try it with him. Mobbs responded with a threat to knock Coaley's head off should he try anything. A tussle ensued which ended when Mobbs charged at Coaley with his knife drawn, aiming at Coaley's side. The affray discontinued when Coaley ran off.

Henry Cave of Little Linford reinforced the evidence given by Coaley regarding the white slop. Cave saw Mobbs on the evening of the murder between seven and eight o'clock and he was no longer wearing the white slop. Cave also identified Mobbs' knife.

A Mr Harris, from Newport Pagnell, described how he had passed Mobbs and his brother on the evening of the murder at around six thirty. Harris asked Mobbs if he knew Thomas Newbury and said what a shock it was that he had been found dead with his throat cut. Mobbs did not respond but the witness thought he looked 'very pale and downcast'.

Mr Worley, coroner, summed up and asked the jury if they thought there was sufficient evidence to commit William Mobbs for trial. The jury took only ten minutes to agree that William Mobbs should stand trial for the wilful murder of Thomas Newbury.

The trial commenced on 10 March 1870. Messrs Byles and Browne led the prosecution while Mr O'Malley Jr defended.

Mr Browne delivered his opening speech to the jury very ably. From what he told them it was hard to see how this was anything other than a straightforward trial. Numerous witnesses would testify that the knife found near the scene with blood on it belonged to Mobbs and the blood-stained white slop that was also found near the scene was the one Mobbs had been wearing that day.

The piece of evidence not immediately available to the prosecution was a valid motive. All the evidence pointed to Mobbs as the killer, but what had been his motivation? What had driven him to brutally murder a ten-year-old boy? Was it simply a petty squabble after all?

When the surgeon Mr Rogers gave his evidence it was challenged by Mr O'Malley as it did not accurately concur with the statements he made at the coroner's and magisterial inquests. At the trial, Rogers deposed that the wounds seemed like a 'dragged' wound and not a stab. However, at the previous inquests, Rogers had described the wounds to Newbury's throat: 'I found a stab on one side of the throat and the other wound seemed hacked out'. It may be considered that the type of wound inflicted was irrelevant and the only concern to the jury was who had committed them. However, the defence case rested strongly on this evidence, which could be described as inconclusive because of the vagaries in its presentation to the courts. The fact remained that young Thomas Newbury had indeed been killed and O'Malley sought to discredit the surgeon's testimony as inconsistent, contradictory and therefore unreliable.

The case for the defence worsened when John Haycock from Stoke Goldington testified that he had saw Mobbs fire off his gun near the freeboard around half-past three on the day of the murder, firmly putting Mobbs at the murder scene at the appropriate time. Mobbs used the gun, which only fired blanks, to keeps birds from the crops. Eli Warren, also of Stoke Goldington, recalled seeing Mobbs in the vicinity around the same time.

Mr O'Malley mounted a considerable defence in light of the mountain of evidence against his client, hoping to secure just the merest crumb of reasonable doubt in the jury's minds and spare his client the hangman's noose. O'Malley asked that Joseph Staunton be recalled. Staunton testified that when he had discovered Thomas Newbury's body, he had noticed that the boy's throat had been cut. O'Malley asked Staunton if he'd given the same testimony previously at the magisterial inquest to which Staunton replied he had. O'Malley then proceeded to quote Staunton's evidence recorded in the transcript of the inquest: 'When I first noticed the body I did not notice that there was a gash in the throat.' Clearly, this called into question the reliability of another important witness who had given conflicting evidence under oath.

The witness asserted that he had told the inquest that he noticed a cut and had demonstrated with his hand where the cut was and replicated this action at the trial. O'Malley had managed to prove that two of the witnesses, including the highly educated surgeon, had delivered unreliable testimony.

Mr Browne, prosecuting, then addressed the jury, albeit briefly, because to the majority of spectators this appeared to be a straightforward case. Browne implied that O'Malley's questioning of the surgeon, Mr Rogers, was an attempt to convince the jury that this was not a case of wilful murder but one of self-defence after Mobbs and Newbury had fought. He instructed the jury that they could not believe this fantasy if they accepted the testimony of the surgeon, for the wounds he described were not consistent with those inflicted in a tussle. Browne reminded the jury that Thomas Newbury had been described by his employer as a weakly boy of only ten years of age and could hardly have resisted in a fight with the healthy twenty-year-old Mobbs.

The prosecution rested and Mr O'Malley made one further eloquent plea to the jury with his closing speech to acquit his client. He told them that because a body is found with brutal injuries this did not necessarily mean the crime was that of wilful murder or had indeed been perpetrated by a man at all.

O'Malley asserted that the evidence presented only proved that Mobbs may have killed the boy, for there were no witnesses present who observed the attack and if he had in fact killed the boy, again there was no one present who had witnessed the circumstances. The only person present who knew what had happened was William Mobbs. To this end, the jury could not be certain of the circumstances surrounding Thomas Newbury's death. They would have to carefully consider whether Mobbs had killed the boy and if they believed this, they would have to return a verdict of manslaughter for they knew not what led to poor boy's death. He went further, claiming that they would have to consider acquittal if it was not conclusively proven without any doubt that Mobbs was responsible.

No witness had been produced who could testify to any disharmony or resentment between the accused and the victim so what possible reason could Mobbs have had for brutally murdering his young friend and colleague? Therefore the jury's task was simple. If they were not convinced Mobbs had killed Newbury they must acquit him. If they were not convinced it was murder without any reason, then they must find him guilty of manslaughter and not of wilful murder.

The judge's comprehensive and unbiased summing up followed. He retold the evidence that he considered indisputable and directed the jurys toward its responsibility with regard to the verdict they would return. He included the lesser charge of manslaughter, going so far as to tell them the accused man's death would be on their consciences. However, it was his belief that if they believed Mobbs was responsible for Newbury's death, they should return a verdict of wilful murder and not manslaughter.

The jury retired for fifteen minutes before they returned a verdict of guilty of wilful murder but with a recommendation of leniency due to the age of the accused. The judge donned the black cap and passed sentence:

William Mobbs, the jury have discharged a very public duty. You have been found guilty of wilful murder on the most pregnant and conclusive evidence. The Jury have accompanied their verdict with an earnest recommendation to mercy on account of your youth. That recommendation I shall forward to the proper quarter but you must prepare to die. The sentence of the court upon you is that you be taken from here to the place whence you came, that you be hanged by the neck until you are dead and may the Lord have mercy upon your soul. Your body will be buried within the precincts of the gaol.

On 28 March 1870, Williams Mobbs was hanged at Aylesbury Gaol, his penalty for the wilful murder of Thomas Newbury.

On the Thursday preceding his execution he wrote a letter to James Newbury's father expressing his sorrow and regret for the death of his son and asked for his forgiveness.

The following day, he had a final meeting with his immediate family members and prepared himself for his inevitable fate.

The diminutive Mobbs (he was only 5ft tall) made a full confession in the presence of Messrs Rawson and Tindal, the latter of whom recorded it and read it back to him:

I, William Mobbs, declare that when I saw the boy Newbury coming towards me I felt all of a shake and as if I could not help murdering him. I had dreamed of murders and I had seen a picture of the man Baker murdering the girl in the hop garden. It was a very hot day and we sat down together on the freeboard. Newbury laid down and about ten minutes after we met it was done. I rolled over him and when over him I cut his throat twice. He halloed out 'Oh' only once. I felt as if I did not know where I was or what I was doing. I went away bird-keeping. I left the body where it was. I put my smock where the police found it. I had no grudge against the boy and I never had a quarrel or struggle with him. When we were sitting on the ground I asked him what they would say if anybody was to kill him and he (Newbury) said they would hang him. I replied 'what hang him for killing varmints?' He said 'yes'. Upon this I immediately attacked Newbury. I had a book about Cain and Abel in my dinner basket. That book was given me by my grand-father just before he died. It belonged to my uncle Thomas Joyce, my mother's brother.

The picture Mobbs refers to in his confession was from a sensational murder that took place in August three years earlier. It was the infamous murder of the eight-year-old Fanny Adams at the hands of Frederick Baker. Baker, twenty-nine, was a solicitor's clerk who had carried Fanny into a hop field and struck her over the head with a stone. Fortunately for Fanny, this blow was the wound responsible for her death for Baker then mutilated the body. He removed the legs and the head even going as far as to remove the eyes from their sockets. The torso was opened and the internal organs were removed and scattered (it took a number of days to recover all the contents).

Mobbs' execution was witnessed by the undersheriff Mr Tindal, gaol officials and members of the press. Around 100 people gathered outside the prison to wait for the raising of the black flag above the prison gates to signify the sentence had duly been enacted.

Shortly after eight o'clock in the morning, Mobbs was led from his cell attended by Rawson the chaplain and his entourage, reading from the Bible as he did so.

As Mobbs approached the gallows along a corridor he was met by William Calcraft, who was to be his executioner, and was pinioned in the usual fashion to preclude any struggle once the lever, sending the condemned man to his fate, was pulled.

Mobbs appeared to have his mind elsewhere, as if he was already passing into the next world and did not seem to fully comprehend the scene around him. Perhaps he was resigned to his fate and accepted it.

In a swift display of efficiency, Calcraft covered Mobbs' head with a hood, attached the rope to a ring suspended from the beam and delivered the unfortunate man out of this world. This was the first execution conducted within the walls of Aylesbury Gaol. As was the procedure, the body was left to hang for an hour despite death resulting from strangulation in under a minute.

The chaplain declared that he had spent much time with Mobbs since his imprisonment and he truly believed Mobbs was repentant and felt great remorse for his crime.

Robert Ceely, the gaol surgeon who was in attendance in his official capacity, confirmed Mobbs was dead. Ceely House in Aylesbury (the building now housing the Buckinghamshire County Museum) is named after Robert Ceely, one of the founding surgeons of the Royal Bucks Hospital designed by Florence Nightingale, where he gave his time without recompense.

'THE MOUTH OF A RIGHTEOUS MAN IS A WELL OF LIFE'

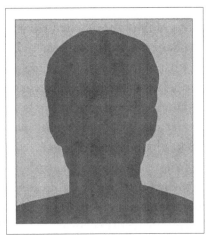

Denham

Suspect:	John Owen
Age:	38
Charge:	Murder

The *Bucks Herald* described it as a 'Sickening Tragedy'. In the early hours of Sunday, 22 May 1870, almost an entire family was viciously murdered in their home in the quaint Buckinghamshire village of Denham.

An intelligent and able mechanic, engineer and blacksmith by the name of Emanuel Marshall, aged thirty-five, lived in a detached cottage at Cheapside near the Oxford Road with his wife Charlotte, thirty-four, his mother Mary, seventy-seven, and his four children.

Mr Marshall's sister, Mary Ann Marshall, thirty-two, was shortly to be married, so the youngest of their children was despatched to Uxbridge in order to allow room for the bride-to-be. Saturday, 21 May 1870 appeared to pass as usual as members of the Marshall family had been observed going about their business as normal. However, none of the family was seen on the Sunday or Monday and the cottage appeared to be closed up, with the windows remaining shut during the day.

Around six o'clock in the evening on Monday 23 May, Mary Ann Sparks, the dead man's sister-in-law, noticed the house was locked up and all the doors and windows closed. She asked a labourer called Charles Alderman to force the front door open. The room was saturated with blood and

The site of the Marshalls' home at Cheapside. (Author's collection)

on the floor in front of them lay the lifeless bodies of Mrs Marshall and Mr Marshall's sister, who had both had their heads bludgeoned.

They investigated further and in a back room discovered the bodies of Mr Marshall's mother and the three children who had remained in the house; Mary, Theresa and Gertrude aged eight, six and four respectively. They had suffered similar head injuries to the adults, with two of the children having their heads completely smashed in.

'The room was saturated with blood'

Mr Marshall was found in his workshop adjoining the cottage. He too had received devastating head wounds leaving his skull shattered. The murder weapons used to inflict such catastrophic injuries were a sledgehammer and an axe, both of which were soaked with blood. Also recovered at the scene was a poker which had been used with such force it had broken apart.

Mr Marshall's body was tidily blanketed beneath an apron, a coat and some sacking. All of the victims, except Mrs Marshall and Mr Marshall, were in their night attire and all the beds displayed signs they had been occupied and vacated in a hurry.

The initial assumptions of those who surveyed the scene were that Mr Marshall had murdered his family and then committed suicide. Fortunately the arrival of two doctors, MacNamara and Ferris, and their subsequent inspection of the bodies confirmed that Mr Marshall was not the culprit after all, as it was impossible for him to have injured himself in the way that led to his death. It was also considered at the time, somewhat erroneously, that one person alone could not have committed so many murders.

It appears Mr Marshall was the first slain. He was at work in his workshop when he was accosted. A struggle ensued and he was eventually subdued by a series of blows to the head with a sledgehammer. The murderer then hid and waited to see if the commotion had roused the attentions of those in the cottage. The attacker then entered the cottage and killed two of the children, Mary and Theresa, in the back kitchen using an axe to smash in their heads. Mr Marshall's wife and sister were killed in the front parlour and Marshall's mother and the four-year-old Gertrude were killed in another room.

A bricklayer named Charles Coombs, who lodged at Charlotte Balham's in Uxbridge, provided information to the police leading them to a suspect known as John Owen, who also lodged at the same address. He had become suspicious of Owen after he had told Coombs he had taken a watch and a chain. Owen was also suddenly wearing much finer clothes which he claimed his brother had given to him. Coombs disbelieved this as he knew Owen did not have any kin in the area. He knew where Owen had fled to and gave the police the address of the Oxford Arms, Silver Street in Reading.

Coombs accompanied Superintendent Dunham to Reading where they found Owen in the tramps' kitchen of the Oxford Arms. Owen, an itinerant blacksmith, was arrested and detained on suspicion of the murders of seven people but not before he offered potentially fatal resistance. Owen saw the police coming and attempted to pull his gun on them. Fortunately, the police descended swiftly and prevented him from discharging the firearm.

The police expected to find Mr Marshall's watch in Owen's possession but were disappointed in this regard. However, equally as incriminating they found a pawn ticket for a shop in Uxbridge owned by Mr Butcher. The ticket was issued in receipt for a watch and some items of clothing. Further incriminating evidence was identified in the clothes the apprehended suspect was wearing. His boots and trousers had been stolen from Mr Marshall. Owen did not deny they were the murdered man's clothes and, in fact, agreed they were Marshall's. Owen said he was present at the murders but had not participated.

The suspect, John Owen, thirty-eight, was a modest 5ft 7in tall, with dark eyes, dark hair and a full beard and spoke with a Scottish accent, although some claimed he had roots in Birmingham. He denied any involvement in the killings but claimed to know the identity of the murderer. Owen was to be transferred to Slough on the 8.10 train from Reading and news of this soon spread, with a crowd in excess of 1,000 people gathering to catch a glimpse of the suspected murderer of seven people.

The governor of Reading Gaol identified John Owen as having served twice at the prison previously. Owen had served eighteen months hard labour for stealing a lamb in Abingdon and had been imprisoned another time for stealing a barrow from a cemetery. In addition to these two bouts of incarceration, Owen had served a third term at Reading and two more at Oxford under various aliases including Jones, Reynolds and Jenkins. In fact, two warders appear to have provided the police with the motive for Marshall's murder at the hands of John Owen. Upon release from Reading Gaol he had told the warders he would not return to prison as he was owed money by Mr Marshall in Denham and should he not him pay his due, he would kill him.

While he was held in custody, Owen displayed continued indifference to the difficulty he now found himself. His composure did falter upon his transfer to the railway station as the restless crowd that awaited him hissed and booed from all quarters. When the train departed, it slowly passed the agitated onlookers who took a second opportunity to verbally abuse Owen.

Another man was arrested in High Wycombe. He was suspected of being an accomplice as he was divulging details of the case in a public house and had been in Uxbridge on the Monday, leaving suddenly in the same fashion as the accused. John Robinson of Silver Street, Windsor, was released without charge two days later as there was no evidence linking him to the crime.

The coroner's inquest began on Monday, 30 May 1870, at the Swan tavern, Denham, before the coroner, Mr Charsley. Police Constable Charles Tavener of Denham deposed that he last saw Mr Marshall alive on Saturday morning outside his shop which was connected to his cottage.

Early on Sunday morning at around three o'clock, Tavener encountered a man, now known to be Owen, in the vicinity of Marshall's cottage. Owen told Tavener that he was there because he had heard a man threatening to throw his wife into the canal. Nothing further happened but Owen swore he would have treated the man in a similar fashion had it done so.

Later, Constable Tavener was called to the Marshall's home following the discovery of the murdered family. He recounted what he saw and how

The Swan, where the coroner's inquest took place. (Author's collection)

the adults appeared to be have been covered up but the children left as they were. Some of the bodies showed signs of being moved and he located the axe and the sledgehammer, both of which were 'out of place' and saturated with blood. Tavener also told how the house did not have the appearance of being robbed but that drawers containing clothes had been opened and clothes strewn about. They were of similar size and style to those worn by the stranger he had seen on Sunday morning. This was an important point because there were some clothes left in the bedroom that did not appear to be Mr Marshall's and were stained with blood and splattered with pieces of brain. So it was evident that the murderer had changed out of his bloodstained clothes in order to evade detection and left them at the murder scene.

The police investigation, under the lead of Inspector Sutton, was still ongoing so he asked permission to withhold any further evidence, as it may be prejudicial to any trial or future developments – it was still considered there may have been an accomplice. The coroner accepted this point and the inquest proceeded.

Charlotte Marshall's brother, Job Spark, was unable to identify the watch that had been pawned by Owen at Uxbridge, but he did identify the chain that was regularly worn by his sister.

Mary Ann's fiancé, George Amor, had expected to visit Denham for their wedding but shortly found himself giving evidence before the inquest. He was unable to offer any information relevant to the murders; this was not unexpected as he had just learned of the terrible fate of his intended wife and did not live in the locale.

The coroner's inquest adjourned until Friday, 3 June 1870. In the meantime, the magisterial inquest was conducted in Slough. Superintendent Dunham described the murder scene as he had found it and the events surrounding Owen's arrest. The evidence was punctuated by Owen interrupting the inquest, contradicting the statements made by Dunham and those of subsequent witnesses.

The man who had tipped off the police as to John Owen's identity and guilt, told the inquest that he was aware Owen had pawned the watch and sold some of the clothes he had stolen from Mr Marshall. Crucially, the blood-stained clothes found discarded in the Marshall's cottage were identified as belonging to Owen. Additionally, the clothes stolen from Marshall's bedroom, some of which had been pawned in Uxbridge, were identified as those worn by the accused when he was arrested.

The accused continued to interrupt at regular intervals which resulted in him being permitted to put questions to the witnesses. This concluded only when the accused could not remember the questions he wished to ask.

John Owen was charged with wilful murder and was to be conveyed immediately to Aylesbury Gaol. The transfer aroused a great deal of interest, resulting in a gathering crowd with many calling for Owen to be lynched. At the railway station, Owen was rushed into the ticket office, where those accompanying him encountered great difficulty closing the doors against the crowd, which had surged forward in an attempt to dispense their own summary justice. This was not the end of the matter. The mass of people clamouring for blood rose into the hundreds. For seven long minutes the police were under siege and the crowd made several concerted efforts to seize Owen to save the judicial system the bother of trying him.

The police were seriously overwhelmed and outnumbered so elected to use stealth to rescue the precarious situation they found themselves in. Some of the police boarded the train and as it departed, they hung from the windows looking back at the station. The station announcer then told the crowds that the prisoner had left the station and they should disperse. The disappointed crowd rapidly dissolved, allowing the police to smuggle Owen onto a goods train which met the departed passenger train further down the line where they boarded it unhindered.

During the journey, Owen boasted that he intended to escape in order to avoid being hanged. The entourage arrived safely at Aylesbury where only a small number of people knew of Owen's impending arrival. He was swiftly transferred to the gaol to await his trial.

The bodies of the slain family were buried on 3 June 1870 at five o'clock at Denham churchyard before a huge congregation. Marshall's mother was interred with her husband who had died some years before. The remaining six members of the family were buried together in a single grave.

John Owen did not have to wait long for his trial which started on 20 July 1870, less than two months after the murders of seven people. In the interim, it had been voiced in many quarters that Emanuel Marshall had two

St Mary's church, Denham, where all seven victims were buried. (Author's collection)

The grave containing six of the victims. (Author's collection)

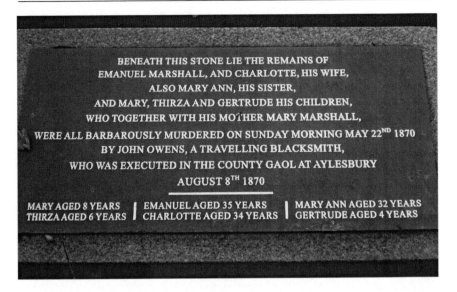

BENEATH THIS STONE LIE THE REMAINS OF
EMANUEL MARSHALL, AND CHARLOTTE, HIS WIFE,
ALSO MARY ANN, HIS SISTER,
AND MARY, THIRZA AND GERTRUDE HIS CHILDREN,
WHO TOGETHER WITH HIS MOTHER MARY MARSHALL,
WERE ALL BARBAROUSLY MURDERED ON SUNDAY MORNING MAY 22ND 1870
BY JOHN OWENS, A TRAVELLING BLACKSMITH,
WHO WAS EXECUTED IN THE COUNTY GAOL AT AYLESBURY
AUGUST 8TH 1870

| MARY AGED 8 YEARS | EMANUEL AGED 35 YEARS | MARY ANN AGED 32 YEARS |
| THIRZA AGED 6 YEARS | CHARLOTTE AGED 34 YEARS | GERTRUDE AGED 4 YEARS |

A plaque displaying the inscription on the gravestone. (Author's collection)

brothers, both of whom had emigrated. One had died but the other returned and was known as John Jenkins, one of Owen's aliases. Owen had been observed visiting Marshall on a number of occasions. So could it be that Owen killed seven members of his own family including his own infant nieces?

The trial, presided over by Judge Channell, attracted the same frenzied interest the initial reports and inquests had, with crowds arriving at the court and pandemonium ensuing as many more than the court could hold attempted to secure a seat. The police were present in large numbers and formed barriers to prevent access to anyone further, once the courtroom and adjoining rooms were full to bursting. Most had to be content with waiting outside.

It appears Owen's true identity had still not been established as he was addressed in court by the name of Jones. He stood accused of the wilful murders of seven members of the Marshall family to which he pleaded not guilty. Messrs O'Malley and Metcalfe appeared for the prosecution, while Dr Abdy defended.

Mr O'Malley began with the opening speech telling the jury that guilt in this case was indisputable. He covered the evidence already provided in this chapter but also introduced further details. He would call two witnesses,

Charles Coombs, who had led the police to the accused, and Charlotte Balham, who saw the clothes the accused wore on the Saturday night. Owen had told Belham and Coombs he was going away which they thought odd as he had only just asked for lodgings there in Uxbridge.

Another witness would be called; Elizabeth Simpson, also of Cheapside in Denham, had been outside early on the Sunday morning searching for a lost key. She saw the accused man emerging from the Marshalls' house and not knowing Mr Marshall, she supposed it was him. The man told her the same story he told Constable Tavener regarding an argument he had witnessed between a husband and wife. Simpson also revealed how during her conversation with Owen, he told her he had not been in Denham for six years and it was only then that she realised it wasn't Mr Marshall. She asked who he was as she had seen him leave the Marshall house but Owen replied only to claim that the Marshalls had gone away on holiday.

The prosecution also introduced further evidence concerning the pistol with which Owen attempted to evade arrest. It was one of a pair, the other being found at the Marshall house.

Another witness called for the prosecution was a carman (a carrier) named Henry Salter. Salter gave Owen a lift on the Sunday evening from Denham. Owen told Salter that he had no money but his brother did and he would have some of it, but not until after dark.

James Weston, of Butcher's Pawn Brokers, identified Owen as the man who sold him a watch and chain taken from the Marshalls' house. Owen had used the pseudonym of George Wilson, resident of Reading. Numerous witnesses from Reading deposed that Owen had a key with him when he was at the Oxford Arms after the murders. Owen gave the key to Harriett Willis who was employed there, who in turn gave it to Superintendent Jarvis. Jarvis tried the key in the lock of the Marshall house and it fitted perfectly. There were paint splatters on the key and the lock that were identical.

The defence's case was, at best, flimsy. There was a mass of evidence against Owen. Dr Abdy had little ammunition with which to fuel any remote doubts the jurors may have harboured. He delivered a lengthy closing speech in which he relied heavily on Owen's genial demeanour following the murders. After all, how could anyone who had committed seven murders in one night continue as if he had merely spent the evening indulging in idle pastimes? Abdy also claimed there were no witnesses who saw Owen enter or exit the house. This did not signify anything as the house is set back from the road and the closest neighbour was around 100 yards away. Plus, there was the testimony of Mrs Simpson who claimed to have seen Owen leave the house and had engaged him in conversation assuming he was Mr Marshall.

The judge also delivered a lengthy summing up before asking the jury to retire to consider their verdict. The jury returned after just two minutes such was the weight of evidence against Owen, with the only verdict one could have expected – guilty. Owen was asked if he knew of any reason why a sentence of death should not be passed upon him, to which he simply replied, 'Nothing.'

Judge Channell then placed the black cap upon his head and pronounced a sentence of death on John Owen for the murder of Emanuel Marshall in the parish of Denham. Strangely, the only indictment for which Owen was tried was that of the murder of Mr Marshall, but the judge told Owen that it was safe to assume he was responsible for the deaths of the remaining six victims. Only Marshall's son, who had been staying in Uxbridge, had escaped with his life. However, he had been parted forever from his parents, grandmother, aunt and siblings. When the judge had concluded, Owen, somewhat flamboyantly, thanked him. The people gathered in the courtroom then began to jeer the condemned man who looked up half-smiling. Owen then attempted to speak to one of the witnesses but was whisked away immediately.

The 8 August is an auspicious day in the calendar, one that is supposed to bring luck. For John Owen, or whoever he truly was, it brought anything but fortune for he had an appointment with the hangman.

Since the trial, further information had surfaced pertaining to the motive for the unscrupulous attack. Owen had worked for Mr Marshall some years before but had caused damage to some wheels he was working on belonging to a local farmer. As Marshall could not claim his fee for the damaged wheels he refused to pay Owen who was responsible for burning them. Owen bore a grudge against Marshall for this reason and this is why he attacked and killed Marshall and then six members of his family. This corresponds with claims Owen made to numerous people shortly before the murders that someone owed him money and if he did not get it he would kill the man.

In custody, unlike the other condemned men in this book who awaited the same terrible fate with pious devotion, Owen remained as aloof and uninterested as he always was. Reverend Bunbery, the prison chaplain, was very attentive but Owen dismissed his overtures to repentance. Owen declared that he was a Catholic so a priest of that denomination attended him but he was met with the same callous indifference.

He was visited by his wife who implored him to make a full confession of the crime. This Owen agreed to do in the presence of the Revd Joshua Greaves of Great Missenden. However, the confession, which was recorded in full, was considered so wrought with falsehoods that he was not asked to sign it.

Owen went on to receive many visitors, including ministers of numerous denominations, but he continued in his customary nonchalant fashion. All of them entreated him to make a confession and ask forgiveness from God but he was unrepentant. In an effort to display his disdain for those around him and the fate he awaited, he asked to see his coffin and that he be permitted to sleep in it the last two nights before he was to be executed.

The executioner was William Calcraft, an experienced professional at his macabre and unusual craft. Owen demanded Calcraft visit him immediately but when he did not, Owen threatened he would strike Calcraft down if he displayed such impudence on the scaffold.

The day before his execution his demeanour remained unchanged and he refused the last service he would ever have the opportunity to attend. Instead, he engaged in conversation with Calcraft. He was in high spirits and ate and slept well. On the morning of the execution, which, as always, was due at eight o'clock in the morning, he woke around three and told the warders that he was innocent of the crime and had received the clothes from two men at Marshall's cottage. He then spent the rest of his time joking with those around him.

The appointed time arrived and Owen was escorted to the scaffold. Calcraft struggled momentarily with one of the buckles used to pinion the prisoner, so Owen offered to turn to the light to assist him and did so immediately. The buckle was fastened and the ritual commenced. Calcraft shook hands with Owen and withdrew to pull the bolt which would send the man to his death. Owen interrupted the proceedings and asked the Chief Warder, Mr Armitage, if he could address those present. Armitage agreed and Owen spoke to the assembled people. He proclaimed his innocence and feigned forgetting the name of the man for whose murder he had been convicted. The hood was placed over his head, the bolt removed and justice dispensed. Owen died almost instantly with just one violent convulsion.

The black flag at the prison gates was raised to signify to the hundreds gathered there that the execution had taken place.

Some elements of the press who unequivocally supported capital punishment, set the propaganda machine into action, asking what other punishment could be suitable for a monster such as John Owen.

Each year on the anniversary of this terrible crime, an anonymous visitor leaves flowers on the grave containing six members of the Marshall family wiped out over 140 years ago.

CASE SIX 1873

'OUR SORROWS AND OUR TEARS WE POUR'

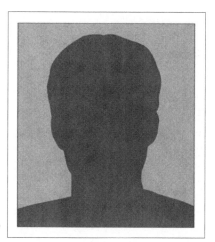

Oving

Suspect:	Henry Evans
Charge:	Murder
Age:	32

The sleepy tranquillity of the gentle and picturesque village of Oving, near Aylesbury in Buckinghamshire, was shattered by a horrific murder which the *Bucks Herald* cited as one of the 'most brutal cases' of murder to ever have occurred in this county.

Henry Evans, a long-time resident of Oving, was apprehended by the police and charged with the wilful murder of his wife Annie Seabrook Evans. Henry was thirty-two years old at the time of the murder, some twelve years younger than his wife. They married at Oving parish church almost nine years before the tragic event. In fact, the couple were just one day away from their ninth wedding anniversary.

Henry Evans earned his living as a pig dealer while his wife, who had lived and worked in Aylesbury until their marriage, continued to contribute a healthy and not unsteady income from her talents as a dressmaker. Indeed, Annie employed a number of people in the undertaking of her business; such was her ability and popularity. Henry and Annie were both well connected and highly respected in the village community.

Initially, the marriage promised to be a contented one, bereft as the happy couple were of the immediate concerns of poverty that blighted

Oving. (Author's collection)

so many marriages in the nineteenth century. However, Henry soon developed a distinct fondness for alcoholic beverages and after only a few years of marriage this induced his suffering wife to complain of his idleness. This led to arguments between the couple eventually leading to the murder of poor Annie.

The detached house they shared in Oving was on the main road with Henry's father, Emanuel Evans, living almost opposite. Their nearest neighbour was a man named Clark whose house rested some 20 yards away. The house was said to be in good order and represented people who were 'well-to-do'. The house was immaculately clean, but all this taste and refinery was attributable to Annie, for Henry's business interests were failing as a result of his drinking and subsequent shiftlessness.

On Saturday, 22 March 1873, between nine and ten o'clock in the morning, Annie was barbarically murdered in the supposed sanctuary of her own home.

Annie had prepared herself for a visit out, finishing off her attractive outfit with a trimmed hat and a pair of woollen gloves. She made off in the direction of the front door along the passageway from the kitchen where she had lingered a moment. The attacker followed Annie down the passage from the kitchen and struck her a thumping blow on the head with a poker.

It was evident the perpetrator of such a hideous attack was a strong male as the force of the blow was catastrophic and judging from the angle of the blow, the man would have been right-handed. The blow did not kill Annie outright and it is certain she was aware of the worse horrors that were to follow. Her survival of this initial assault appears to have induced an insatiable bloodlust in her heartless attacker. He fetched a sizeable and rusty carving knife from the kitchen and proceeded to dash at his stricken and defenceless wife, hacking at her as if she were a butchered animal being dissected for meat. There were gashes to her face but these paled into insignificance when compared to the wounds inflicted upon her throat which almost entirely severed Annie's head from her body. In the process of suffering such a horrendous onslaught of frenzied violence, it appears Annie must have regained consciousness for a time. Three fingers on her right hand were almost severed probably from a futile attempt to protect her throat from the wild slashing of her husband, the very man who should protect her from all ills. He systematically brutalised and slaughtered the woman he loved, married and promised to cherish and protect; reducing her to a bloody and disfigured state.

Once the attack was over and Annie lay motionless on the floor of the hallway of her home, her husband returned to the kitchen with the poker with which he had first struck his wife. Such was the cruelty and force of the blows, the poker – cast of iron – was bent out of shape. After such a violent attack, most people would feel shock or disgust to some degree, especially beating and slashing a life partner slowly to death, yet Henry failed to display the slightest compassion for Annie. Strangely, it appears he possessed the consideration to feed the canary they kept in a birdcage in the house shortly after the attack concluded. This we know because a small quantity of blood-soaked sugar was found in the birdcage.

Henry decided to cover his tracks and deflect the burden of suspicion away from himself and he acted immediately. Clearly remorse, nor guilt, nor shame affected him as he calmly abandoned his wife's bloodied corpse, leaving it to be found some days later.

He discarded the overcoat he was wearing as it was, inevitably, saturated with blood. Naturally, had he ventured out in the overcoat he would not only arouse interest upon the eventual and inevitable discovery of his wife's mutilated body, it would identify him as the most likely killer. Why he left it at the scene remains subject to speculation. In addition to the removal of his overcoat, Henry closed all the internal doors. This way, no one peering in from the windows would be able to see his wife's body on the floor in the hallway. This, he anticipated, would buy him valuable time.

Around eleven o'clock, Henry visited the stable of his father to procure from him the use of a pony and cart on the false pretence of driving himself and Annie to Aylesbury. Emanuel gladly obliged, obviously not suspecting that foul play was afoot.

Henry returned home to discover a neighbour nearby, to whom he expressed utter shock that his wife had gone away and locked up the house leaving him without a key and unable to gain entry. He remained outside his house and proceeded to recite his invented distress to anyone who ventured by. The following two nights were spent at his father's house opposite, as he continued the charade throughout Saturday and Sunday ignoring advice from his father and his neighbours, including Betsy Cannon who was employed by his wife, that he should knock down the front door. Henry cited the exorbitant cost of door locks as the reason against proceeding in this fashion and reiterated his certainty that his wife would soon return and that he would await her arrival.

Annie's sudden disappearance played upon the minds of some of her neighbours who contrived to discover what had become of her. On the afternoon of Monday, 24 March 1873, Henry had vacated the area so the concerned neighbours visited Emanuel Evans. They procured a ladder and it was Emanuel himself who ascended it to look inside through a window above the front door. The closed doors inside the house prevented most natural light from penetrating the hallway where Annie had laid dead for two days but he saw something lying on the floor, indiscernible in the murk. He was not convinced it was a corpse but he immediately felt a sickening feeling and refused to enter the house.

Another man, John Robins, scaled the ladder to look inside. He too was concerned with what he saw and they immediately sent for Constable Edward Earl. Earl arrived with a local blacksmith named Samuel Ward who gained entry to the house. The grotesque sight of Annie's mutilated body awaited them inside, her head against the scullery door and her right hand in a defensive position across her throat. Superintendent Shepherd and the surgeon, Mr Spencer were summoned to the grisly scene.

The immediate suspect was, of course, Henry Evans. He was no longer in Oving, having left earlier that day, so Superintendent Shepherd and Constable Stonnell set off in hot pursuit. They managed to trace him to Leighton Buzzard so they headed in that direction. They got as far as Cublington where Henry was apprehended, almost by accident, as he was making his way back in the direction of Whitchurch and his home in Oving where, unknown to him, his wife's body had been discovered. Constable Stonnell arrested him and relayed him to Winslow lock-up.

Henry denied all knowledge of the crime and any complicity in it but when he was searched he was found to be concealing evidence that would implicate him, more than if he carried the bloodstained murder weapon itself. In one of his pockets was the back door key to his house; the house he

Winslow lock-up, where Henry Evans was initially held. (Courtesy of Terry Foley)

The former Butcher's Arms, where the inquest was held. (Author's collection)

had broadcast to all that he had been locked out of. His handkerchief, along with other sundry items, also appeared to be stained with blood.

Despite his protestations of innocence, his behaviour was not consistent with a man who has just heard of the barbaric slaughter of his wife. Instead, he was preoccupied with evading the eye of suspicion and neglected to show concern or grief for the demise of his wife. Upon being searched at the site where he was apprehended, Henry stated, 'I shall own to it all.'

Annie Evans' body was transferred to the Butcher's Arms in Oving the following day to coincide with the coroner's inquest conducted by Joseph Parrott.

Joseph Parrott, a solicitor of local firm Parrott and Coales, appears to have been an important and respected local man. He was admitted as a solicitor in 1845 and became Clerk to the Guardians, and Superintendent Registrar in 1846. Parrott was one of the coroners for Buckinghamshire, having been appointed in 1847. He was undersheriff for Bucks in 1867, 1869, and from 1878 to 1881 inclusive, and Secretary and Solicitor to the Aylesbury Association for the Protection of Persons and Property from 1848 to 1884.

In attendance at the coroner's inquest were the Chief Constable, Superintendent Shepherd, PS Nobes of Quainton and Captain Drake. The jury, consisting of fourteen men, including the foreman Augustus Guy, viewed Annie Evans' corpse before evidence was heard. Betsy Cannon testified first. She told the court that when she returned to Oving from a couple of days' sabbatical in Aylesbury on Sunday 24 March, she had seen Henry outside his father's house. He told her that Annie had left him on Saturday morning and gone to Aylesbury so he was surprised they had not seen each other there. Cannon was certain Annie was not in Aylesbury as it was her custom to always visit her dear friend Miss Turnham who had only just given Betsy a note to pass on to Annie.

Cannon then recalled how Henry had visited her mother's house before she herself had risen, around eight o'clock on the morning of Monday, 24 March 1873. Cannon did not see Henry herself but her mother told her shortly afterwards that Henry informed her Annie had travelled to Aylesbury on Saturday with a carrier from North Marston by the name of Dick Holden.

Betsy saw Henry about an hour later, again outside his father's house, and told him to visit Dick Holden to discover the truth of his wife's defection. Henry agreed to this and when she saw him again, Henry stated that he had seen Dick in Bowling Alley. Later, however, Cannon's brother met with Dick Holden who denied he had seen Henry at all.

Cannon proved to be a crucial witness as she spent all of her time at the Evans' home, only returning to her own home to sleep. She recalled the previous two years where the comfort which the pair had become accustomed to began to wane as earnings reduced dramatically. Husband and wife began to argue frequently and as a result Mr Evans turned to drink.

Annie had left Henry several times as she could no longer endure his harsh tongue and foul temper, his drinking and his shiftless attitude which brought them debts. In fact, she was in the process of looking for a new home in Aylesbury, the town of her birth.

Constable Earl told the court of how Henry had called him over on the morning he had murdered his wife and asked him if he had seen her. Henry claimed she had gone to Pitchcott and as Earl had passed through there on his way from Quainton asked whether he had seen her, but Earl claimed that he had not.

Bowling Alley, Oving. (Author's collection)

Pitchcott. (Author's collection)

Constable Earl then gave evidence regarding the murder scene. Annie had been dressed to go out, however her hat was not near the body but upon a chair. The hat was dented as if a blow had been struck down upon it and there was a spot of blood present. He recovered a large rusty carving knife from the dresser in the kitchen which was saturated with blood and a poker from the same room, which retained hair and blood along the shaft. The hair was identified as belonging to Annie Evans.

There was no key found in the back door, which was locked, and no signs of forced entry. Henry's overcoat was discovered at the scene covered in blood and had obviously been worn by the killer in the pursuance of the act of murder.

The surgeon from Whitchurch, Mr Spencer, who had attended the murder scene, listed the numerous and extensive injuries sustained by Annie Evans:

> I found three extensive lacerations upon the upper part of the scalp and a fracture and depression of the cranium. One was a comminuted fracture (where the bone is broken into several pieces) and compressed into the skull about an inch. The other wound was not fractured but was driven into the brain injuring it. Another wound I found on the vertex at the back of the head, apparently without fracture. There was a wound on the forehead an inch in extent. All these wounds were on the left side and the left ear was penetrated by a knife. The right ear is also severely cut. On the right side of the face, over the cheek bone, is a contused and penetrating wound. An inch above the orbit is a horizontal wound about an inch in length. It must have been inflicted by terrible violence. On the right side there are two stabs just above the ear as well as two cuts on the ear itself. On the left side there is a deep cut below the angle of the mouth extending to that of the jaw and there is another deep cut on the throat, dividing the larynx and large vessels to the spine. The mouth was firmly closed in consequence of the muscles underneath being severed. The injuries to the skull or those to the throat would either be sufficient to cause death.

Spencer then confirmed that the weapons produced in court, the rusty carving knife and the poker, were utterly consistent with the injuries just described.

The day's business concluded with the foreman of the jury asking about the discovery of the key in Henry's possession which implied he could have come and gone as he pleased. The inquest was adjourned until Thursday.

The 25 March arrived and the inquest recommenced at the Butcher's Arms in Oving. It was sadly remarked by those present that the body of the Annie Evans, which had been so badly mutilated, still lay in the same state since Tuesday. No coffin or order of internment had been arranged during the interlude in proceedings, which caused great consternation to those gathered in the public house.

Esther Hindley, a school mistress from Oving who practised the harmonium at the Evans' House, testified that she visited Annie on a daily basis and had noticed relations between Henry and Annie worsen over the last twelve months. Henry had done no business in that time. He borrowed £3 from Annie in order to purchase some pigs but instead used the money to pay a debt he owed to his father. When Esther left Annie on the evening before she was murdered, she noted that Annie and Henry appeared to be on good terms. She saw Annie again the following morning (less than thirty minutes before she was murdered) when she dropped in on her way to Aylesbury.

Hindley identified Henry's coat and the back door key. She then recounted her conversations with Henry Evans on the Saturday some time after eleven o'clock. Contrary to what Henry had told Betsy Cannon – that Annie had gone to Aylesbury with Dick Holden – Henry told Hindley that Annie had gone to Pitchcott to see Mrs Dancer. Henry then claimed that he saw his wife later going through the village and had called after her. She offered him the key but he declined it.

The coroner asked if Hindley had ever heard any threats made between Henry and Annie. She responded in the negative; however, she did state that Henry had sworn to kill himself by slashing his own throat if she left him.

Hindley was with Betsy Cannon on the Saturday morning when Henry said his wife was in Aylesbury but she and Cannon had just returned from Aylesbury and did not see her there. Henry changed his story saying she had gone to Pitchcott instead.

Henry Evans' father gave his evidence next. It was a task that took its toll on an aging and frail man who was compelled to participate in his son's murder trial. Apart from confirming points already covered, he told the court that he thought Henry and Annie had quarrelled again and that Annie would return in a few days time, as she had done before. Emanuel Evans recalled how his son decided to go to Maynes Hill to look for Annie as this was where she often worked, so he hitched up his pony and cart and set off. That was the last Emanuel saw of his son until after he was arrested.

The coroner, Joseph Parrott, summed up and advised the jury they did not have to decide if Henry Evans was guilty, only that there was a good case against him. Parrott also advised that in this case, with such overwhelming evidence against the accused, it was difficult to observe any other outcome. The jury retired only briefly before announcing a unanimous guilty verdict of wilful murder.

The trial for what became notorious as 'The Oving Murder' commenced on 18 July 1873. Messrs Merewether and Atthawes appeared for the prosecution while Messrs O'Malley QC and O'Malley junior defended the accused. The jury, consisting of twelve men, were sworn in.

Maynes Hill. (Author's collection)

All Saints, Oving, where Annie and Henry were married and Annie was buried. (Author's collection)

Despite the enormity of the physical and circumstantial evidence, and his claim to the police, 'I shall own to it all,' Henry Evans pleaded not guilty to the charge of wilful murder. This was presumably an understandable but futile attempt at depriving the hangman of his morning's work.

Henry's aunt was called as a witness, telling the court she had been to see Annie at around nine thirty on the Saturday morning. At that time Annie was still alive and not yet dressed for leaving the house. But it was Henry Holden who provided more crucial evidence. He recalled seeing Henry walking away from his back door at eleven o'clock on the morning of the murder. Although he could not confirm if Henry had closed the door, he did notice Henry carrying a red stained handkerchief. He also believed Henry had been drinking, judging by his agitated appearance and demeanour.

Henry told Holden that Annie had gone to Pitchcott to Mrs Dancer's house to meet Mrs Flowers from Padbury. He saw Henry again later in the

The graveyard at All Saints. (Author's collection)

day and was told by him that he had gone to Mrs Dancer's and neither she nor Mrs Flowers had seen his wife. This part of the accused's story was true as confirmed by Martha Thorne who was at Mrs Dancer's house when Henry called asking for the key.

An Oving labourer by the name of John Smith told Henry that his wife had definitely not gone to Pitchcott. Smith was certain of this because he and a colleague had been working next to the road Annie would have had to travel along to reach her destination.

Constable Earl then told the court his observations of when he inspected the body at the Evans' home. He found that Annie was dressed for going out, with the exception of her hat which was on the chair. It was evident Annie had been wearing the hat at the start of the attack as there was an indentation consistent with a strike from the poker and there was blood on the inside. Henry deposed that there were spots of blood on the ceiling, the walls, the doors, the floor, the carving knife, the poker and a duster recovered from the overcoat left at the scene.

Dr Newham from Winslow then described how he had inspected Henry's clothes after his arrest and found marks of blood, most likely human blood, on every item, although he could not rule out pig's blood being responsible for the stains. Indeed, Henry Evans' father testified that Henry had 'stuck' a pig on the Sunday morning. It was not to be enough to weave any doubt in the jurors' minds, confronted as they were with the overwhelming evidence as well as a confession of sorts made by the accused to the police upon his apprehension. Henry had told the police he was returning to Oving as he knew he had left sorrow behind.

Mr Merewether delivered his closing speech in favour of the prosecution, followed by Mr O'Malley defending. The defence case rested on the question of premeditation. O'Malley contested that as there was no question of premeditation a lesser charge of manslaughter should be brought and not one of wilful murder. In an attempt to highlight that this act of violence had been out of character, O'Malley called three character witnesses, the Revd W.A. Young, a curate from Oving, Joseph Stranks of Aston Abbotts, and John Belgrove a farmer from Oving, to testify to the accused's usual gentle conduct.

The judge summed up, advising the jury that they could not convict Henry for manslaughter as he was not tried on that charge but only on the charge of wilful murder. If they doubted he had committed wilful murder then the prisoner should be acquitted. However, he also displayed surprise at the comments of Mr O'Malley that the jury could not find the accused guilty of wilful murder unless there was conclusive proof of premeditation. The judge instructed the jury that it would set no legal precedent to convict a man for wilful murder, even if premeditation had not been proven, and in any event the penalty of death was equally applicable where it is firmly established there is no premeditation.

He then recited the law on the matter, explaining to the jury that if a man takes another's life by committing actions that are likely to cause him death or intends to cause him death the charge of wilful murder applies. Manslaughter would only apply where the perpetrator could prove beyond reasonable doubt that there were serious mitigating circumstances causing the death, such as self-defence. The judge then apologised if he was appearing prejudiced against the accused, but it was his duty to make the jury aware of the law and Mr O'Malley had misled them on this point.

Therefore, the prisoner was either innocent or guilty of murder. There was no other verdict they could reach. The jury retired for fifteen minutes before returning a verdict of guilty but without premeditation. Mr O'Malley failed to save his client from the gallows. The judge put on the black cap and sentenced Henry, who was clearly distressed, to be hanged until he was dead.

He returned to Aylesbury Gaol to await his sentence. The receiving book at the prison records Henry as being thirty-two years old, 5ft 4in tall with grey eyes and an oval visage. He was assessed to be in good health with no 'lamity' or infectious disease. He had not been held in custody previously and his conduct was described as good.

Mr I.J. Wood of Aylesbury sent a petition to the Home Secretary in order to procure a commutation of the sentence of death to one of transportation. It is hard to see how such a brutal murderer could have received a reprieve of this magnitude and it was dismissed.

Just days before his execution, Henry received his friends and family in his cell to bid them an emotional farewell. Since his resignation to his grim fate, Henry was reported to display regret and sorrow for the terrible crime. He conducted himself in a placid manner, receiving solace in the words of God provided to him by the chaplain. This was reflected in a number of letters he wrote during his incarceration, which illustrated the repentance he now felt. Henry is attributed as saying he feared the scaffold not for the penalty it brings, but for the parting of friends: a profound claim from a man who, without mercy, slaughtered his wife in cold blood. His parting message to his friends was, 'Tell my friends that I am going to Jesus and that I can see the shining angels all around me awaiting my arrival.'

The day before his execution, Henry made a full confession to his father and his friends Ezra Stilton, Aaron Griffith and Thomas Clark who visited him in prison. He said he and his wife had words on the Friday evening in bed. Henry told Annie to be quiet and go to sleep to which she replied, 'You shall have no sleep tonight.' The following morning, Annie was cleaning the grate when she cut her finger. It was from this minor wound that the bloodied sugar was introduced to the canary cage.

Henry claimed he and his wife were getting ready to go to Aylesbury when he came downstairs and was confronted by Annie in the passageway.

Annie was holding a carving knife and said to him, 'Harry, I am tired of my life and intend to do for you before you leave today. For if I kill myself nobody will believe you did it and you will get off.'

According to Henry, he went to his bedroom and locked the door. Annie attempted to force the door but failed and went back downstairs. Worried his wife was ready to harm herself, Henry went back downstairs but Annie confronted him, still holding the carving knife. Afraid for his safety, he went into the workroom and shut the door. Annie forced her way in and he said to his wife, 'If this is the case I must defend myself.' He grabbed the poker which stood nearby and struck her over the head with it. All strength appeared to desert him so he struck her a number of times. She fell backwards into the passage and lost all strength. He took the knife from her hand and in doing so caused the injuries to her hand recited at the trial. The other wounds inflicted upon his wife were caused during the ensuing struggle. Henry dropped to his knees in prayer and cut his wife's throat in order that her suffering would cease. Feeling immediate remorse for the unfortunate demise of his wife he fetched a razor and put it to his throat but did not continue as he thought he heard his father shouting his name. He went to the door to give himself up but there was no one there.

The confession was clearly one of fantasy and desperation of a man frantic for a reprieve. At no point during the inquest or the trial did he make any assertion of self-defence. In fact, it appears to have been an afterthought in light of Mr O'Malley's closing speech and the judge's clarification of the law at his trial.

It was an overcast and grey sky that greeted the bells of St Mary's church, Aylesbury on the morning of Monday, 4 August 1873. Only minutes remained before Henry Evans, now pale and gaunt, received his punishment for the wilful murder of his wife. Henry ascended the scaffold accompanied by the chaplain, who continued to recite words of comfort to the condemned man.

The executioner, George Smith, who was a tall man of good appearance and demeanour, prepared Henry for his fate. After placing the noose around the condemned man's neck he placed a bag over his head, all in the most matter-of-fact fashion. Henry's legs were then strapped together and he was ready to meet his fate. Smith shook hands with Henry as did the two warders in attendance. Finally, the chaplain shook Henry's hand and amid an eerie and unbroken silence the lever was pulled. The chaplain departed with speed, overcome with emotion at the sight he was duty bound to witness.

As was the custom, a black flag was raised over the entrance to the gaol to confirm the execution had been effected. Ten minutes later, Robert Ceely inspected the body to confirm life extinct. Joseph Parrot conducted the inquest that followed.

Reproduced below is the text of the letter Henry Evans wrote to his grief stricken parents just one hour before he was executed:

Aylesbury, August 4 1873.

My dear father and mother and all my friends. I thought, by the help of God, of writing a few lines to you once more, as that is the only thing I can do now on this earth for you. It seems very hard for a child to sit down to write the last words, almost, that he will be able to utter. Oh, my dear father and mother, what a comfort it is to me now, in the last moments of my life, to feel the Lord so gracious to me. I can say, my dear father and mother, this morning I feel the Lord still to be with me, and the nearer I get to the time of death, the more of God's blessed spirit I feel. Oh, my dear father and mother, it won't be long now before I shall have to cross the narrow stream of death. Oh, then I shall leave this world of trouble.

Our sorrows and our tears we pour,
Into the bosom of our God;
He hears us in the mournful hour,
And helps to bear the heavy load.

Then Jesus, my safe ladder art,
To lift me to the skies;
And on it when I find I'm got
My heart begins to rise

To be with Jesus for ever and ever! Oh, I long to be there now, so as I shall be at rest, and out of all my trouble. The trouble of leaving you, my dear father and mother, and those dear friends I love so on this earth, are almost more than I can bear; but I am resting quite alone on Jesus, for strength and support; and I trust my dear father and mother, and all you my dear friends that this is where you are all looking to. For there is no other place under heaven, nor no other name given amongst men, whereby we can be saved. So, my dear father and mother, and friends, as the last words, let me beg of you to meet me in heaven, as that is my home. Good bye! Monday morning, seven o'clock. This my last words. Jesus is mine – don't weep!

From your loving son,
Henry Evans

'WHOSO SHEDDETH MAN'S BLOOD, BY MAN SHALL HIS BLOOD BE SHED'

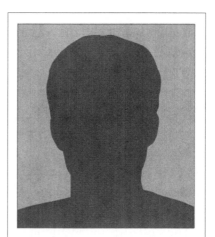

Piddington / Ludgershall

Suspect:	William Dumbleton
Age:	21
Charge:	Murder

Above was the opening lesson delivered by the parish rector following the murder of the man nicknamed 'Gentleman Johnny'; his prediction, if it were one, was to become reality.

At around ten o'clock on the morning of Wednesday, 4 February 1880, an itinerant draper from Berkhamstead by the name of Thomas Plenderleith was travelling along the Ludgershall to Piddington road, when he spied a hat apparently discarded on the ground. As he stooped to pick up the hat his attention was drawn to the ghastly sight of a mutilated corpse lying partially submerged in water in a ditch with his head facing towards the road.

Upon closer inspection, Plenderleith saw that the throat of the lifeless man had been cut from ear to ear with such force that the head was almost entirely decapitated. There were further slashes to the face and evidence of a forceful blow to the head. The draper immediately raised the alarm and the police attended the scene. A search of the area revealed a discarded knife, suspected to be the murder weapon, hidden behind a hedge.

'the ghastly sight of a mutilated corpse'

Plenderleith suggested to the attending Police Inspector, George Webb, that the deceased man looked as if he had been run down by a horse and cart. However, Inspector Webb suspected foul play was afoot in the form of a horrific murder.

The knife was almost immediately identified as belonging to a man known sometimes as Harris, who also went under the pseudonym of Barrett, but was in fact called William Dumbleton. It was also noted that the evening before, Dumbleton had been drinking with the murdered man and three other men, Thomas Gibbons, his son Edwin Gibbons and Thomas Walker in the Seven Stars public house in Piddington not far

The Ludgershall to Piddington road. (Author's collection)

The ditch where John Edmonds' body was found. (Author's collection)

from where the corpse was discovered. The police immediately arrested Dumbleton on suspicion of murder.

William Dumbleton, the man identified as the owner of the murder weapon discovered at the scene, was soon taken into custody.

The victim was initially described as a young man of around thirty-five years of age who left behind him a wife, and an aging father. But no further details were divulged pending the police investigation. The murdered man was, in fact, thirty-six years of age and was a local living in Ludgershall.

The slain man's body was removed to the White Hart public house in Ludgershall to await the coroner's inquest. This was conducted by Joseph Parrott on Friday, 6 February 1880, at the National Schoolroom in Ludgershall. The police were represented at the inquest by Superintendent Shepherd, while Joseph Kingham adopted the role of foreman for the jury.

Proceedings opened with Joseph Parrott, the coroner, advising the jury that it would be unlikely they would complete the hearing that day and that they would need to be recalled.

The Seven Stars public house, Piddington. (Author's collection)

Firstly, they would need to adjourn to the White Hart to view the corpse of John Edmonds, a diminutive man known to his friends as 'Gentleman Johnny'.

Thomas Plenderleith was the first witness called to give evidence upon the jury's return to the schoolroom. He confirmed that on 3 February he had stayed the night at the White Hart public house and departed the following morning, around nine forty-five, to travel from Ludgershall to Piddington. At around ten past ten he had travelled about a mile and was only half a mile from his destination. He had stopped to pick up an abandoned hat in apparently good condition and looked around for the owner expecting to find them nearby. What he discovered was infinitely more macabre and sinister. The body of a man he could not identify lay motionless, protruding from a ditch that ran alongside Norman's Field.

Plenderleith raised the head of the stricken man to confirm he was dead and then continued to Piddington to raise the alarm. In Piddington, Plenderleith spoke to Messrs Chester and Sulstone, a baker and a

The former White Hart public house in Ludgershall. (Author's collection)

The former National Schoolroom in Ludgershall. (Author's collection)

wheelwright respectively. Constable Gibbons was sent for and the group returned to Norman's Field.

There were signs of a struggle on the opposite side of the road to where the body lay and a smear of blood almost 2 yards long. Other blood splatters were present, along with evidence that the body had been dragged to its current location. Two masses of clotted blood were also observed on the grass near to the body.

John Jordan Sulstone, the wheelwright from Piddington, was the next witness to give evidence. Sulstone corroborated the evidence given by Plenderleith. He recalled that Mr Chester, the baker, had lifted the body from the ground enabling Sulstone to identify the corpse of John Edmonds lately of Ludgershall. Edmonds was a watch repairer and a member of the Ludgershall Friendly Society. Together, Sulstone and Chester removed the body from the water in which it was partially submerged and saw that the victim's throat had been cut.

Sulstone proceeded to search the body. He noticed one pocket was unbuttoned and one pocket lay outside the trousers. He found a silver

Norman's field. (Author's collection)

Ludgershall village. (Author's collection)

hunter watch, two beans, a few small nails and a knife. These were placed in a leather bag belonging to Edmonds found nearby and handed to the police. Mr Chester, meanwhile, sent a boy to fetch Inspector Webb.

Shortly after, a surgeon arrived at the scene to inspect the corpse. Inspector Webb duly attended and despatched men present to procure a horse and cart to transport the body to the White Hart at Ludgershall. In the meantime, Sulstone accompanied Inspector Webb to Piddington to visit the homes of Thomas and Edwin Gibbons and Thomas Walker who were known to have been drinking with the victim on the evening prior to his murder.

Webb and Sulstone first visited the house of Thomas and Edwin Gibbons in which Webb made a thorough search for any incriminating evidence. Only Edwin Gibbons was at home during the search and under questioning from Inspector Webb, he immediately began to lie. He denied being out the evening before, assuring Webb that he had been home by seven in the evening. However, Webb knew this to be untrue and pressed Gibbons further, whereupon he confirmed he had been in the public house until much later.

Sulstone and Webb then went to question William Dumbleton, who was labouring in a field at Clew Hill Farm, which belonged to a local man named Paxton. Like Edwin Gibbons, Dumbleton also lied about his whereabouts the evening before, stating that he had been at home. Webb again countered this by telling Dumbleton that he was known to have spent the evening in the Seven Stars public house. Dumbleton confirmed this to be true.

After leaving Dumbleton, Webb and Sulstone returned to the murder scene to search the adjacent field owned by Mr Holt, where they hit upon the good fortune of discovering a discarded knife spotted with blood.

The next person called was James Munday who was the landlord of the Seven Stars inn at Piddington. He identified William Dumbleton as a patron of his inn. Munday described how Dumbleton had been in the Seven Stars at around seven in the evening and had apparently been asleep in a corner. Munday chatted about work with Dumbleton (James Munday was also a carpenter/joiner) before Dumbleton moved on to join Thomas Walker, Thomas Gibbons, Edwin Gibbons and John Edmonds. Munday asserted that in his opinion, Dumbleton was quite sober and had consumed only nine pennyworth of drink during the evening. Dumbleton, along with the other members of the group, left together at around ten o'clock.

Munday went on to say that he had witnessed Edmonds with two watches, one of which Munday himself inspected. One belonged to Edmonds while the other belonged to a local man named Edward 'Neddy' Faulkner. The other members of the group also saw the watches. Munday concluded by stating the men were friends and there was no apparent animosity among them.

Dumbleton's brother, Albert gave his evidence next. Albert Dumbleton shared a house in Piddington with his father and the accused. Albert had not seen his brother on the night of the murder, having retired for the evening around nine o'clock. He confirmed that William did own a pocketknife, which he had found in Mr Brown's field last harvest time. The knife was white with the bone missing from one side of the handle and originally had three blades but one had broken off. The point of one of the remaining blades had also broken.

Then it was Inspector Webb's turn. He recounted the events that followed the discovery of the body. He stated that when he found William Dumbleton he was sitting in a field at Clew Hill Farm (about a mile south-west of Piddington) consuming his dinner. Webb asked to inspect the knife with which he ate his repast and then searched Dumbleton but found nothing of relevance. However, Webb did find bloodstains on Dumbleton's clothing. Inspector Webb challenged Dumbleton to account for the blood and in reply Dumbleton said he had scratched his hand that morning whilst 'cutting a scraper' from a hedge. Webb asked who he had been working with so he could confirm this claim and the accused offered the name of Robert Wiggins. Dumbleton protested that Wiggins would not know he had cut himself but he would be able to confirm the work he was doing when the injury was suffered. Webb posited that the amount of blood on Dumbleton's clothing was too much for the scratch present on his hand. Dumbleton was duly arrested and relayed to the Seven Stars under the escort of a policeman.

Clew Hill Farm. (Author's collection)

Webb then went with John Sulstone to the field owned by Mr Holt to search for the knife which was subsequently found. The knife was located in a hedge not far from where Edmonds' body had lain. The knife was closed up and had not been opened since.

William James Bond was called next. Bond was the surgeon who had inspected the body soon after Thomas Plenderleith raised the alarm. He described, at length, the injuries sustained by Edmonds:

I found one wound extending from two inches below the left ear on the left side across the throat to the other ear, altogether about nine inches long. This wound at the commencement was very deep, cutting the windpipe on the left-hand side, passing on to the right dividing the superficial muscles but leaving the artery and veins intact. There is another wound commencing at the angle of the jaw on the left-hand side going to within an inch of the centre of the jaw on the same side, then passing by the angle of the mouth on the left side where the under lip is severed passing down almost an inch under the lower lip to about an inch under the centre of the jaw. I should think the wounds were caused by rather a blunt instrument. There is also a mark above the left eye like a bruise and there is a scalp wound on the right side of the head about two inches long, which I should think was produced by a fall upon a stone. There are three bruises to the arm two below the elbow and one above. The wound in the throat was the cause of death. The wounds were certainly not as would be caused by the deceased himself. The knife produced [Dumbleton's white pocketknife was produced as an exhibit for the prosecution] would be a very likely instrument to cause the wounds and the blood on the knife is of recent date. When I first saw the body I should think the deceased had been dead from ten to twelve hours, that being generally about the time required for bodies to get stiff and cold in cases of sudden death and the body was quite stiff when I saw it.

Evidence concluded with John William Mole identifying the body of John Edmonds whom he had known since childhood. The hearing was then adjourned for a week.

During the inquest sabbatical, three events of note occurred. Firstly, the funeral of John 'Gentleman Johnny' Edmonds took place on Monday, 9 February 1880, with his body being buried in the churchyard of the parish church. The congregation was sparse and consisted almost entirely of family members. The second noteworthy event was the magisterial inquiry at Brill Police Court which was conducted in front of a panel of magistrates on Tuesday, 10 February 1880. Mr H. Bode and the Revd R.H. Pigott received evidence, much the same as heard previously on the first day of the coroner's inquest. Dumbleton was charged with wilful murder and was remanded in custody for a further week.

Thirdly, on the same day that the magisterial inquiry took place, the watch belonging to Edward Faulkner that Edmonds had shown to fellow patrons in the Seven Stars, and for which the theft from his person had resulted in his brutal murder, was discovered by Constable Avery of Brill police station. Avery had been despatched to search the area around Dumbleton's house to see if he could discover any incriminating evidence.

The parish church at Ludgershall, where John Edmonds is buried. (Author's collection)

Indeed, that is exactly what he found, for concealed within a thatched roof of an outbuilding in the garden, used by the accused and his family, was a pocket watch. This was later identified as belonging to Faulkner and the one carried by Edmonds on the evening he was murdered.

Dumbleton was oblivious to the discovery of the watch and in the meantime attempted to co-operate more fully. On Thursday, 12 February 1880, he asked Inspector Webb for permission to walk from Brill, where he was remanded in custody to Piddington, accompanied by Constable Avery. Dumbleton declared his intentions honestly, for not only did he claim the walk would serve him well, but that he would recover the stolen pocket watch. Inspector Webb asked to which watch Dumbleton alluded. The accused replied, 'The one Edmonds lost,' he continued, 'I had that and hid it and will show you where it is if you will take me down.'

The adjourned coroner's inquest resumed on the somewhat inauspicious day of Friday, 13 February 1880. Joseph Parrott resumed his role as coroner and recalled James Munday who was the publican at the Seven Stars in Piddington. Munday asserted that Edmonds had two watches in his possession on the evening of his murder. He concluded by declaring the group of men including the Gibbonses, Dumbleton, Walker and Edmonds were all sober upon their departure from his hostelry.

Thomas Gibbons, a labourer from Piddington, gave evidence next concerning the events of the evening as they unfolded inside the Seven Stars. Gibbons claimed Edmonds had produced two watches, although he himself had not held them as he had been on a different side of the room. However, he did witness Thomas Walker, James Munday and William Dumbleton handling the watches. The men left the public house together just before ten o'clock and it was foggy outside. Gibbons, with his son Edwin and the murder victim, John Edmonds, walked together as far as the school. Dumbleton and Thomas Walker did not accompany them. It is assumed Walker travelled in the opposite direction while Dumbleton waited near the gates of the Seven Stars. The Gibbonses left Edmonds at the road to enter their home and Edmonds continued along the Ludgershall road. Thomas' son Edwin, who was also a labourer in Piddington, shared the same house. He gave an almost identical account of the evening but asserted that had Dumbleton been returning home after leaving the public house he would have walked the same route as he and his father. Edwin, however, did not see where Dumbleton actually went.

The remaining member of the group was Thomas Walker and he was called next. Walker was also a Piddington labourer, which is probably why the men all knew each other, but with the exception of the familial tie between the Gibbonses, none were close friends. Walker had no real information to offer as he had travelled in the opposite direction, leaving the group outside the public house. He did state that he and Dumbleton spoke for a few minutes outside the Seven Stars before Walker set off for home and Dumbleton made his way along the road in the direction of the Gibbonses and John Edmonds. Thomas Walker did hear either Edwin or Thomas Gibbons bid Edmonds a good evening once the Gibbonses had reached the front gate of their house.

Constable Avery described how he, Inspector Webb and other policemen had searched the area around Dumbleton's home including various outhouses and the wall skirting the property. He noticed a

The crossroads in Piddington, where the Gibbons left John Edmonds the night he was murdered. (Author's collection)

Piddington village. (Author's collection)

thatched roof on a small building used for storing wood and coal, also doubling as a privy, and perceived a number of holes probably caused by nesting birds. One of the holes looked freshly disturbed so he ventured in a hand. He located a silver hunter watch with a steel chain from which hung a watch key, some tokens and a farthing. The watch was produced in evidence. The building was some 32 yards from the Dumbletons' cottage and was actually situated on the land of a carrier by the name of Henry Judge. This detail was later confirmed by William Dumbleton's brother Albert, who was recalled and described the Dumbleton cottage as having no privy whatsoever on the premises but that they used the one in the ownership of Henry Judge.

Edward Faulkner, known locally as Neddy, was a labourer from Ludgershall. He was the owner of the pocket watch, and on 20 January 1880, he retained the services of Edmonds as his watch was in some minor need of repair. He identified the watch produced as evidence by Constable Avery as belonging to him and described the small faults present upon it.

Esau Reynolds, yet another labourer from Piddington, deposed that he had been a work colleague of Dumbleton's at Clew Hill Farm. He had borrowed the white pocketknife with the broken blade to eat his lunch with two weeks before the murder. Reynolds had been working with Dumbleton on the morning of the murder and recalled Dumbleton wearing a white jacket and corduroy trousers, neither of which showed bloodstains.

Dumbleton's sister Anne, who was just eighteen, was summoned to provide her evidence next. Anne shared the cottage with her brothers and identified the white pocketknife as belonging to her brother William. She last saw it two or three weeks prior to the inquest. It was at this time a second knife was produced in evidence; this one was a black-handled kitchen knife. Anne identified this knife also and said it was her mother's and was kept in a cupboard at the Dumbleton family home.

A distraught Maria Edmonds, wife of the deceased, was next on the witness stand. She asserted that her husband had left their home in Ludgershall on the morning of 3 February at half past nine in the morning and carried with him two watches, one of which was his own, the other belonged to Edward Faulkner. He was hired to clean a timepiece for John Faulkner in Ludgershall. Maria Edmonds never saw her husband alive again.

Robert Wiggins, William Dumbleton's workmate from the garden allotments at Clew Hill Farm, was recalled but contradicted the statement made by Dumbleton that he would confirm Dumbleton had been working on 'cutting a scraper from a hedge'. This evidence was crucially important to Dumbleton as he had asserted this was how he had bloodied his clothing and although Wiggins would not know of his wound, he would be able to confirm the work he undertook that led to the injury.

Dumbleton had earlier attempted to explain away the advanced drying of the blood and ensuing darkness due to his rubbing tobacco into the stain. Wiggins recalled how he had a chance meeting with Dumbleton around ten to seven on the morning after the murder, near the outhouse where the watch was found. Dumbleton was carrying a spade. Wiggins finished by declaring he never noticed any scratches on Dumbleton's hand.

The inquest was adjourned again until the following Tuesday when the magisterial inquiry was also due to resume.

Tuesday 17 February saw the resumption of the coroner's inquest ahead of its magisterial counterpart, with the surgeon William James Bond the first to give evidence. Bond had made a microscopical examination of the bloodstains on Dumbleton's clothing and was certain that all the stains originated from mammals, with the exception of one fowl stain on his jacket.

Constable Avery's evidence was read to the court and a member of the jury asked Avery if at any time Dumbleton had offered any indication to him of the whereabouts of the missing watch. Avery denied that any intimation had been given to him by Dumbleton or any other person. Avery then described a conversation he had with Dumbleton the Tuesday before, immediately following the magisterial inquest. Dumbleton claimed he was innocent of the murder of John Edmonds but he knew some important information pertaining to the crime. He then made the following claims to Avery:

As I stood against the gate of my home, the chap came up to me and said 'let us go and see if old Johnny has got money'. I replied 'no I are not going after him'. He said 'Oh come on' and then started off and I followed behind him. He went faster than me and 'catched' Johnny. When I got near to them I heard a scuffle and started off running. I then said 'did you hear Johnny halloa?' and he replied 'no I did not hear him halloa'. When I got there the other man had got him down trying to cut his throat with his own knife but he could not do anything with it. He said to me 'lend me your knife' and I leant it to him and he soon finished him. He offered me my knife back and I said I shan't have that thing now. Then the other person searched Edmonds' pockets but he could only find one watch. I don't know if he found any money or not. Then I catched hold under Edmonds' arms and helped to carry him into the ditch where we left him. The other person offered me the watch and said 'here take this, that will be about fair'. I took it and going along I thought to myself this watch is no use to me, I don't know what to do with it so I hid it going home.

Constable Thorne, in whose custody Dumbleton had remained since his arrest and transport to Brill police station, delivered some new evidence previously unheard before any inquest. On Thursday, 12 February 1880, Thorne had gone to Dumbleton's cell where Dumbleton complained of feeling 'very dull' and gave the following statement:

On the night of the murder I was at the public house. We all left together at ten o'clock at closing time. After I got out into the road opposite the public house I stayed there for two or three minutes: I then left for going home. As I was going down the road I saw a man getting over the wall at Munday's [Seven Stars] close into the road. He called out to me and asked who they were that went down the road. I said Edmonds and others. He said 'let's go and see what Johnny's got on him'. I made no answer the first time. He then asked me again and I went with him. He asked me if I had a knife and I said yes. He said 'does it cut well?' I said 'yes'. He said 'lend it to me for mine is no more good than a wooden one'. We then followed after Edmonds and about 50 yards before we overtook him the other man ran on and left me. I stayed behind the hedge whilst the other man knocked him down. I then went up to them. When I got there he had cut his throat. The other man offered me my knife. I said 'I shan't have it for it is all blood'. He then threw it over the hedge. After we had given him enough we both took hold of him and threw him the other side of the road and chucked him in the ditch. Whilst I was helping in carrying him across the road, I fell down twice going over the road. We then made a promise if either of us was found out not to split about the other one and after I have made a promise I will suffer the law before I split about him.

The coroner summed up and asked the jury to decide whether there was sufficient evidence to commit the accused for trial. After a brief deliberation and without the court being cleared, the jury returned a verdict of wilful murder against William Dumbleton.

The magisterial inquiry resumed at a crowded Brill Police Court following the end of the coroner's inquest, again ably presided over by Mr H. Bode and the Revd R.H. Pigott. It was remarked upon that Dumbleton's demeanour was a continuance of the sullen mood previously displayed.

Much of the evidence presented at the coroner's inquest and the previous convening of the magisterial inquest was repeated. Maria Edmonds, wife of the deceased, asserted that her husband had left home with 3s and 6d in silver upon his person. No money was found on the body when it was recovered. She had not raised the alarm when her husband did not return home that night, although she had expected him, because she thought he had spent the night in Bicester. The watch had been repaired and Edmonds had expected to receive payment for it that day. Edward Faulkner, next up, confirmed Edmonds had not returned the watch to him.

Robert Wiggins, Dumbleton's workmate, gave a much fuller deposition to the magisterial inquest than he provided to the coroner's inquest. Wiggins claimed that when he and Dumbleton commenced working on the morning after the murder, he had no knowledge of Edmonds' demise until Inspector Webb took Dumbleton into custody at around one o'clock that afternoon.

In the meantime, they had indulged in what the witness described as a rather one-way conversation regarding living honestly and within the word of the Lord. Dumbleton appeared distant and loathe to chattering. More importantly, Wiggins recounted how they discussed Edmonds' condition in the Seven Stars the previous evening. Dumbleton did discuss with Wiggins the drunken state Edmonds was in the night before and he had warned him that it was a dangerous road to travel (Piddington to Ludgershall) in such a parlous condition.

Wiggins appeared to corroborate Dumbleton's claim that Edmonds was drunk on the night he was murdered, stating that Edmonds was sleepy from consuming too much beer.

After some confusion over evidence being presented by Constable Thorne, the inquest was closed, but not before Dumbleton was formally charged with the crime of wilful murder. Dumbleton elected to remain silent when given the opportunity to reply to the charge. He was then transported from Brill to Aylesbury Gaol to await trial at the next assizes.

Despite the offence taking place in the county of Buckinghamshire (it was just inside the parish of Ludgershall), the trial for what was now dubbed, somewhat notoriously, the Ludgershall Murder, was held at the

Crown Court at the Northampton Assizes on 17 April 1880 before Justice Lindley. The indictment of John Dumbleton was clear. He would stand trial for the wilful murder of John Edmonds at Ludgershall on 3 February 1880. The prosecution team was made up of Messrs Bullock & Tindal while the presiding judge appointed Mr Kennedy as defence counsel.

The trial, despite the necessity of readdressing the evidence already deposed at the earlier inquests, did introduce new evidence and a new witness, the relevant highlights of which we shall now address. Of course, it was completely necessary for the jury to hear all the relevant testimony placed before the coroner's and magisterial inquests respectively, but it was also imperative that the witnesses were available for professional cross-examination and witnesses for the defence were able to be called.

Mr Bullock started proceedings with his opening speech for the prosecution. Surprisingly, Bullock claimed that the doctor had deposed Edmonds' artery had been severed although in fact, the surgeon William James Bond had actually stated at the coroner's inquest that, 'This wound at the commencement was very deep, cutting the windpipe on the left-hand side, passing on to the right dividing the superficial muscles but leaving the artery and veins intact.' Bullock also claimed that he believed circumstantial evidence to be more often reliable than direct evidence, a somewhat bewildering claim as direct evidence can provide a definitive suspect, whereas circumstantial may offer a candidate who is guilty of little more than meeting a specified set of criteria that may apply to any number of people.

Bullock then addressed Dumbleton's claim of the involvement of another man. While Bullock did not accept the involvement of a third party, he highlighted the legal viewpoint that Dumbleton's actions, as described by him, still merited the same charge and any ensuing punishment if he were found guilty.

Bullock was making some rather flamboyant assertions to convince the jury of Dumbleton's guilt on the basis that he had almost certainly been present at or around the time of the murder. Dumbleton was to alter his version of events a number of times; are we to believe he eventually confessed to the crime because he felt a compulsion to do so, or was he adhering to his promise to the 'other man' that he would not give him up to the authorities?

Inspector Webb told the court that when he first encountered William Dumbleton at his work place at Clew Hill Farm, he had no intention of apprehending him for he had no evidence thus far that separated him from the other men he had spoken to. However, his attention had been drawn to the blood on Dumbleton's clothes and it was for this he was arrested. Dumbleton claimed the blood was from a blackbird he had killed but this was later disputed by the surgeon William James Bond who said only one bloodstain was consistent with that of a bird. Had Dumbleton given Webb a more plausible reason for the blood on his clothes, he would not have been arrested at that time.

The cross-examination appears to have been rather lacklustre, almost to the effect of merely confirming minor details rather than any attempt to instil doubts in the minds of the jurors. In some instances the cross-examination seems to have served the prosecution better than the defence. An example of this is when Mr Kennedy – defence counsel – cross-examined Robert Wiggins who was working with Dumbleton on the morning after the murder. Kennedy merely asked if Dumbleton had the scratch he had claimed to have had on his hand, which was responsible for the blood spots on his clothing, and if he knew of Edmonds' death at this time. Wiggins replied that he saw no such scratch on Dumbleton's hand, nor did he see him cutting a scrape, contradicting Dumbleton's claims to the contrary. He also confirmed that he did not know of Edmonds' death at the time. This latter point seems somewhat irrelevant and would best serve the prosecution rather than the defence.

Albert Dumbleton gave a more comprehensive account of their living arrangements and the knives. He deposed that the white-handled pocketknife belonged to William and saw it in his possession the Sunday before the murder. The black-handled knife which William had been using to eat his dinner when he was confronted by Inspector Webb the day after the murder was identified as belonging to their mother. The house in which they lived had only one bedroom, which was shared by William, Albert, their mother and two sisters. Albert had retired around nine o'clock on the evening of the murder and at that time William had not returned home. When he awoke around six the following morning, William was in the bed he shared with Albert, but Albert had not noticed him when he got in.

Ann Dumbleton also identified the knives, declaring that the murder weapon, the white-handled knife, had previously belonged to her and she had used it to trim her brother's toe nails. She had given it to her brother William when he had lost his own knife some three weeks before the murder. The black-handled knife was her mother's and they had not realised it was missing until Inspector Webb showed it to them. The implication made by the prosecution was that having discarded his own knife in the field following the murder of Edmonds, Dumbleton had had recourse to procure a replacement, which he had done by taking his mother's black-handled knife from the cupboard where it was kept.

Esau Reynolds, a labourer who worked with Dumbleton at Clew Hill Farm, testified that he had borrowed the white-handled knife from the accused to eat his dinner and identified the exhibit produced in court as that same knife. Under cross-examination he stated that he never heard a bad word said of Dumbleton before the murder and had always considered him to be a 'peaceably disposed man'.

Some rather striking evidence was provided by the Surgeon William James Bond. Previously, at the coroner's inquest, Bond had stated that the wound that led to Edmonds' death was the slash across the throat which had cut the windpipe but left the 'artery and veins intact'. However, at the trial and under oath, Bond said, 'On turning the deceased over, I found a very large wound on the throat which had severed the left artery and was the cause of death'. This is utterly inconsistent and why did his evidence change?

Bond then introduced evidence concerning the cut on Dumbleton's hand. He inspected the wound that Dumbleton claimed he had incurred the morning after the murder whilst cutting in a hedge. His work colleague who toiled with him that morning had already claimed he saw no cut to Dumbleton's hand that day. The surgeon Bond then asserted that the cut on Dumbleton's hand was some days old.

Bond continued with his contradictory evidence when he stated, 'If the blood had proceeded from an artery it would be in spots. If it was from a cut hand I would expect it to be smeared'. This evidence is irrelevant if we consider Bond's previous testimony where he reported that the artery had not been cut. He was then cross-examined by Mr Kennedy and claimed, 'the blood from the severance of an artery would spurt out with force'. While this is certainly factual is it relevant?

James Sharpe was the person identified as the 'other man' who had been with Dumbleton at the murder of John Edmonds and he was present in the courtroom. The prosecutors decided they should not call him and the case for the prosecution drew to a close.

The defence counsel, Mr Kennedy, also elected not to call James Sharpe. A surprising move as he may have been able to introduce some doubt into the minds of the jurors as to who had actually killed Edmonds and, therefore, whether or not the killing element was premeditated. Maybe Kennedy accepted the prosecution's allusion that even if someone else had committed the murder, Dumbleton was automatically guilty by association. The judge also felt it was unnecessary to call Sharpe to give evidence. Until this time, the existence of another man had always been viewed as fantasy, but here in court was the man Dumbleton claimed was involved and yet neither the defence nor prosecution questioned him.

Mr Kennedy then addressed the court with a dynamic closing summary. He cited that Dumbleton had been questioned without counsel and appeared at the coroner's and magisterial inquests also without counsel, as he had not the means to appoint one; Kennedy had only himself been appointed to represent Dumbleton at the order of the trial judge, Justice Lindley. He highlighted the evidence against Dumbleton as being entirely circumstantial in nature and this may lead to different interpretations of it. He argued that although there was some credence in Bullock's claims, that circumstantial evidence might prove more cogent that direct evidence, it would necessarily be an unbroken chain of circumstantial evidence to prove reliable. It was true that Dumbleton may have been motivated to steal the man's watch, but to cut a man's throat for it was another matter entirely. More importantly, if the motive was robbery why did Dumbleton, if he *was* the murderer, leave the second watch on the body? He was aware Edmonds carried two watches for he had seen Edmonds with them in the public house that same evening, whereas Sharpe didn't. Kennedy contended that a large number of other men had seen the watches throughout the course of the evening so they were all potential suspects too. He asked the court if they believed it possible for a man who had committed a crime so out of character and inconsistent with his nature, to have continued with his work the following morning as normal, as if nothing exceptional had happened to him.

He then moved on to the blood spots on Dumbleton's clothing. The blood, described by Bond as being of mammalian origin, could not be distinguished between human and any other mammal. Additionally, the blood on Dumbleton's clothing was in spots rather than drenched, as one would expect from the gushing of blood Bond asserted would have resulted from a severed artery.

Kennedy then pursued the avenue of intent. Had Dumbleton set out to murder Edmonds? It was Kennedy's belief that when asked by James Sharpe to see what Johnny carried upon him that was not an invitation to robbery or murder, but more a suggestion of a prank or a jape. Dumbleton was described as an ignorant and illiterate man and should therefore not be judged by the standards of the more educated people assembled in the jury. It was perfectly feasible, therefore, that Sharpe had committed the murder and Dumbleton had come up after and in a panic helped to conceal the body. The defence rested after pleading to the jury to consider all the circumstances with all the facts.

Justice Lindley then summed up, beginning by stating that it was inconceivable the dead man had considered suicide (or self-murder as it was often referred to). He directed the jury to consider the circumstantial evidence and to not discount it, but to consider the probabilities. He disputed the defence's argument that had Dumbleton been the murderer and thief, he would have stolen both the watches, claiming this would apply to whoever had murdered Edmonds. However, this assertion is feeble at best because if Sharpe was the guilty man he would not necessarily know of the second watch, as he had not been present in the public house and Dumbleton, in the heat of the moment, may not have been thinking lucidly enough to consider the theft of the second watch.

The jury retired for thirty minutes before returning a guilty verdict. The judge asked Dumbleton if he had anything to say before sentence of death was passed but he made no comment. Justice Lindley applied the black cap and addressed the accused man:

William Dumbleton you have been found guilty of murdering this poor man and I don't think that anybody who has attended to the case could have expected a different verdict nor would any other verdict really have been consistent with the facts proved in evidence. The jury have thought it proper to recommend you to mercy upon the ground of the way in which you have been brought up and that recommendation will be transmitted in due course to those who are the proper authorities to consider that recommendation. I am bound by law to pass a sentence of death upon you and shall not add to your misery by making any unnecessary remarks. I shall merely pass the sentence that I am compelled to pass and shall leave it to those who will have charge of you hereafter to do whatever they can for you during the remainder of the time you have to live. The sentence of the court is that you should be taken from hence to the place from whence you came and from thence to a place of execution and you be there hanged by the neck until you shall be dead that your body shall be buried within the precincts of the prison of which you were last confined after your conviction and may the Lord have mercy on your soul.

For William Dumbleton, sentenced to be hanged for the wilful murder of John 'Gentleman Johnny' Edmonds, the date of execution came only too quickly. The 10 May 1880 soon arrived, with the time of execution set for eight o'clock in the morning at the County Gaol in Aylesbury. In attendance, along with the usual officials, were the press and no one further.

The tragic man made this final confession on the morning of his execution in front of two witnesses, the governor Mr T. Sealy and the chaplain H.G. Layton:

As God is my witness in whose presence I am about to appear, I declare these my last words before I die. And the statement I made to the chaplain is perfectly true concerning the murder of the poor man. I never thought of doing any harm to the man until James Sharpe jumped over the wall as I was going home. He said, 'Let us go and see what Johnny has got.' He knocked him down. The man (Johnny) said, 'What do you want?' Sharpe said, 'We must finish him while we are about it or we will both be found out – lend us your knife,' but instead of giving him the knife I cut his throat myself. I don't say this from any ill-feeling to Sharpe for I have none at all, but I wish to tell the truth and I hope God will forgive me for my dreadful sin. If I had not been took I believe I should have given myself up. I was so miserable to think I had done such a terrible thing to a poor fellow I had no ill-will against whatsoever. How I came to do it I cannot tell all I can say is it was all the beer. When Sharpe gave me the watch he said it was about fair. What he took I don't know. It is quite true the blood on my clothes was caused by the scratch on my hand. I put the ashes from my pipe on the place which made it look as though it had been a week old. After we threw him into the ditch, Sharpe kicked him in the head.

No more than eighty 'spectators' stood outside the prison to await confirmation of William Dumbleton's demise. This was confirmed with the raising of a black flag over the gates of Aylesbury Gaol upon the drop of Dumbleton's trembling body. The hangman, Marwood, showed the condemned man more mercy than was shown to the victim as death was instantaneous. The body was left to hang for an hour still, as was the custom in executions of this type, before it was cut down for an inquest. The inquest was necessary following the abolition of public executions as surety for the public that the sentence had been duly carried out.

The inquest commenced at twelve noon under the jurisdiction of Mr Worley, coroner. The jury's responsibility was to witness the lifeless corpse of William Dumbleton and confirm the sentence had been carried out against the condemned man and that he was, in fact, deceased.

Joseph Parrott witnessed the execution of William Dumbleton in his capacity of undersheriff. He was tasked with displaying the official document to the jury. The document described the sentence and contained the usual edict that the body was to be buried within the prison precincts, which meant in unconsecrated ground. Mr Parrott confirmed he had witnessed the execution of the condemned man and had previously seen him at the coroner's inquest and the trial.

The gaol surgeon, Robert Ceely, testified that he had been present at the execution and examined the body once it had been cut down, pronouncing life expired. The jury was content that the execution had been carried out in full compliance with the law. Dumbleton was then removed to his earthly grave to await his fate in the next world.

The execution of William Dumbleton at Aylesbury Gaol was to be the last carried out at that location.

On Saturday, 24 April 1880, *The Times* featured a letter written by the magistrate Randolphe Pigott, who had attended the chaired magisterial inquest, pleading for mercy for the convicted man on the basis of his impoverished upbringing as an illegitimate child of a base and crude woman.

It appears that William Dumbleton did not receive a fair trial. It is true that there was a coroner's inquest, followed by a magisterial inquest, which was duly followed by the County Court trial. However, the defence of the witness appears to have been conducted with indifference and the evidence provided to the various courts, sometimes by highly educated witnesses, appears to be inconsistent and contradictory. This does not mean that Dumbleton was an innocent man, but is it possible that once he realised he was likely to hang for the crime, he decided to keep his promise to the 'other man' and not give him up? Did a murderer or a murderer's accomplice walk free? The balance of probabilities points to Dumbleton as the lone attacker, especially in light of his dallying outside the public house when the other men walked along the road in the direction of Dumbleton's own cottage. Perhaps Dumbleton had a meeting arranged with the 'other man' in some preconceived plan to relieve John 'Gentleman Johnny' of his valuable watch. Maybe Dumbleton had not considered murder at all until the deed was done? There are so many questions we will never be able to answer.

At the magisterial inquiry the police made a hash of their evidence, especially when it came to Constable Esau Thorne's and Constable James Avery's respective testimonies.

Constable Thorne had not taken down the statement (reproduced verbatim earlier in this chapter) concerning Dumbleton's confession in his cell, where he implicated another person responsible for Edmonds' death, until Saturday, 14 February 1880, two days after he alleged it was made. He had not previously included it in the evidence he gave to the coroner's inquest, despite claiming earlier in his evidence that he had done so. This induced the Revd R.H. Pigott to enquire as to why this evidence had not previously been given. Thorne's flimsy reply was that he had not thought this evidence was required. The bench asked if Thorne had asked Dumbleton the name of the 'other man' which Thorne denied. Dumbleton disputed this and stated that Constable Thorne had asked him the name of the 'other man'.

Constable Avery then recited the statement where he had discussed the 'missing' watch with Dumbleton. This statement, like that given by Constable Thorne, had not been presented to the coroner's inquest. The bench halted the proceedings and retired briefly to discuss the apparently 'new' evidence now being proffered by the two police constables.

Upon the resumption of the inquest, the bench recalled Constable Thorne and asked if anyone else had been present during his conversations with the accused. Thorne confirmed no one else was present.

Constable Avery then resumed and attempted to recite conversations he had conducted with the prisoner but the chairman of the bench refused to take any further evidence from the police on the basis that it had not previously been declared or recorded at the time. It is important to remember that the coroner's inquest does not only aim to ascertain the cause and means of death, but to commit the accused for trial, assuming that there is sufficient evidence.

Captain Drake, the Chief Constable for Buckinghamshire, who was present purely in the capacity of a spectator, was then forced to step in to advise that the police wished to present no further evidence.

Despite the magistrates' robust intention for a fair trial and the withdrawal of the police evidence at that time, the statement given by Constable Avery that had concerned the magistrates was later given in evidence at Dumbleton's trial and reiterated in the prosecution's closing summary and the judge's direction to the jury.

Maybe Dumbleton was innocent of murder; maybe James Sharpe was involved to some degree. Perhaps Dumbleton was guilty of all charges but simply received a skewed trial leading one to believe he wasn't guilty after all. Dumbleton did confess to the crime to his chaplain. One thing is certain, despite the jury's plea for clemency, Dumbleton paid for his crimes with his life.

BIBLIOGRAPHY

Books

Gibbs, R., *A History of Aylesbury*, 1971

Newspapers

Birmingham Daily Post
Jackson's Oxford Journal
Lloyd's Weekly Newspaper
The Bucks Herald
The Morning Post
The Times

Other Sources

Aylesbury Gaol Receiving Book, 1873

Visit our website and discover thousands of other History Press books.

www.thehistorypress.co.uk

Lightning Source UK Ltd.
Milton Keynes UK
UKOW03f0149110114

224367UK00003B/8/P